Haunted Theatres of East Sussex

Haunted Theatres of East Sussex

Tina Lakin

Frontispiece: Spirits and monsters lurk in the stormy seas off the coast of Hastings.

First published 2008
Reprinted 2019

The History Press Ltd
97 St George's Place, Cheltenham,
Gloucestershire, GL50 3QB
www.thehistorypress.co.uk

© Tina Lakin, 2008

The right of Tina Lakin to be identified as the Author
of this work has been asserted in accordance with the
Copyrights, Designs and Patents Act 1988.

All rights reserved. No part of this book may be reprinted
or reproduced or utilised in any form or by any electronic,
mechanical or other means, now known or hereafter invented,
including photocopying and recording, or in any information
storage or retrieval system, without the permission in writing
from the Publishers.
British Library Cataloguing in Publication Data.
A catalogue record for this book is available from the British Library.

ISBN 978 0 7524 4755 1

Typesetting and origination by The History Press Ltd.
Printed in Great Britain by TJ International Ltd, Padstow, Cornwall.

ACKNOWLEDGEMENTS

I would like to say a huge thank you for the help of several people in the writing and compilation of this, my third book of spooky stuff! To Jonnie White (jpw10@brighton.ac.uk, http://www.flickr.com/photos/velsfi/) and Ben Herbert (www.benjaminherbert.com, contact@benjaminherbert.com), photographers extraordinaire for their beautiful images throughout the book; to Shelley at Hastings Reference Library for the yesteryear images used; to fellow author Anthony Cassar and his wife Geltrude, our dear friends from Malts; to my friend Ewa for ongoing immense support and encouragement which has helped me when I have almost given up; and to my wonderful hubby, John, for being you and putting up with my ghostly goings-on.

CONTENTS

Introduction — 9

1. Music Halls — 11
2. The History of Theatre — 13
3. Seaford — 17
4. St Leonards — 19
5. Rye — 21
6. Lewes — 24
7. Hailsham — 28
8. Hastings — 33
9. Eastbourne — 52
10. Bexhill — 60
11. Brighton — 69
12. Battle — 93

INTRODUCTION

Theatres are places where so many emotions and feelings are played out; they are places of disguise and drama, where people can play at being a different character; where a unique atmosphere is created of illusion; for song, magic and glamour. It is the theatre where large numbers of people mingle from all walks of life, so it is no doubt that some have chosen to linger on and make themselves known in one strange way or another.

Wandering around a theatre or cinema auditorium in the dark can be a spooky experience in itself; add to that the fascinating histories of hundreds of years and stories of murder, jealousy, illicit goings-on and the glamorous lifestyle of those involved within the theatre, and it is not hard to imagine that they are the scenes of the most haunted places in the world. Let your dreams and imagination run away with you and escape into another world for a short time.

The following stories are a collection of captivating and magical tales from the world of theatre and cinema combined with their own unique, and in some cases bizarre, history.

During my journeys around East Sussex researching tales of a spooky nature, I discovered some hidden treasures from both the past and modern-day Sussex. From the quaint chocolate-box villages of Brede and Peasmarsh, the medieval gem of Rye to the Regency splendours of Brighton and Hove, no town was left unturned in my search to find haunted auditoriums.

During my quest I was saddened to learn of the demise of many old theatres, many have been completely lost and forgotten. This is a shame as many were built with love and in ornate design and it is hard to imagine why they were not preserved.

The coastal resort towns of Hastings, Bexhill, Eastbourne and Brighton were like magnets to holidaymakers; the piers along the coast suddenly developed with theatres; tourism had arrived and the South East coast would never be the same again.

Inland, rural towns and villages had theatres in inns or were hosts to travelling theatre companies and circuses on their village greens.

This is my third collection of creepy goings-on and the more I delve into this delightful world, the more I enjoy it; I am spurred on to go further and further. My stories and books have reached many and I am always amazed when someone mentions my work. One of these moments this year was to be part of a book signing at my local Waterstone's in Hastings – it was such fun and something I never thought I would do in my wildest dreams. The more I write ghost stories, the more I am drawn to the possibility that there is something more about things that go 'bump in the night' than anyone can explain. Since 1993 ghosts have become a huge part of my life and I consider them to be my friends. I am not afraid of them but feel a certain amount of compassion towards these restless souls.

I often to think back to my secondary school and the one lesson I loathed more than anything was English. My grammar, punctuation, vocabulary and spelling was absolutely appalling and how I managed to pass an exam in the subject is beyond me. I would like to think that one of my English teachers may have picked up one of my books and read a little and enjoyed the spooky tales that they read. Ever since those times at school my dream was to write a book, well I am now on my third ... never give up on anything you wish for because one day it will come true – but usually when you least expect it.

Sit back and enjoy this creepy collection and let me transport you to a time in history of magic, musicals and macabre goings-on and remember ... 'it's behind you!'

Tina Lakin
March 2008

1

MUSIC HALLS

During my research I was amazed to discover just how many music halls there once were around East Sussex.

British taverns have provided entertainment since medieval times. The 1800s saw 'saloons' providing variety acts. Some carried on and built theatres as extensions to their drinking establishments. The Theatre Act of 1843 meant that such establishments could only be licensed if they were run as theatres. The very first music halls were opened in suburban London. Popularity in these establishments grew after the Industrial Revolution as they provided inexpensive entertainment which was accessible to all. As time went on, however, the upper classes too were participating in this form of entertainment and in 1875 there were over 300 music halls in London, with hundreds more across the rest of the United Kingdom. The most popular names were 'the Empire' and 'the Hippodrome'. The music hall was everywhere: in towns up and down the country in dark and dingy basements to grand theatres with ornate decor. They all, however, provided the same vital requirements: a stage, seating and a bar. Early music halls had long tables where customers could eat and drink whilst they were being entertained.

The music and other acts were always popular but so was the liquor. The Temperance Movement were concerned and said that such establishments encouraged drinking of alcohol by all classes and women. Some halls opened which did not offer alcohol but they did not last long. The British public wanted the entertainment, the booze and the atmosphere! The atmosphere in the halls was a unique treat and experience; however there were those who considered them to be dens of iniquity and evil places, encouraging people to drink and watch acts which were ungodly. Another concern was that of the women who worked at the music halls, with some people thinking they were also prostitutes for wanting to work in such a place. They most certainly were not the kind of place where a decent young lady would work!

Most halls kept the performances subdued and suitable for all the family, where everyone could join in with a good sing song. Few stars of the music halls had good voices and it was generally the larger-than-life personalities who could entertain the crowds. Comedy was found in everyday characters that the audience could identify with and this made the appeal of music halls more universal.

The introduction of film meant the sad decline of the music hall however the songs of those times are still kept alive today with many London pubs having regular music-hall nights and sing alongs.

2

THE HISTORY OF THEATRE

There has always been theatre in one form or another. Greek theatres took the form of large hillside amphitheatres, the largest holding up to 20,000 people – they had a unique way of acting and chanted their lines rather than speaking them. Greek theatres date back to around 600 BC and took the form of festivities and feasts with masks being worn to represent different characters. Women were not permitted to act so men had to perform all roles. The audiences adored both tragedy and comedy.

The Romans copied many of the Greeks' ideas of theatre although their acting had a more vigorous style. The early Christian Church did not approve of the Roman style as it was often quite barbaric and even the comedy was of a hard nature. The Romans preferred comedy to tragedy; in Roman theatre, slaves were used as actors and women took minor roles. They introduced chariot racing, gladiator contests and public executions as forms of entertainment which brought about the building of elaborate public theatres. The plays became a little crude in nature and were rather on the violent side which the Church strongly disapproved of it and demanded that all theatres be closed down.

Many say that when the Roman Empire fell it was the street players and animal trainers who kept its memory alive. The Church had much to do with the decline of the Roman Empire but it equally helped in keeping it alive in the Middle Ages. It was determined to make an impact in a world obsessed with pagan ritual and superstition. Church members became involved in plays performed at the front of church buildings and with communities and towns growing rapidly, new town guilds joined the Church and its plays.

Medieval Theatre
The building of theatres was not allowed in Europe during the medieval period but there were many travelling players, jesters and minstrels who kept the crowds entertained and the idea of theatre alive. They told enchanting stories, performed

A jester. (© Claire Forbes)

crazy juggling acts and made puppets to keep the people in good humour. The performed wherever they could and make their own ramshackle stages out of anything they could find. They survived by handing round a hat in which to collect a few coins at the end of a performance. The Church however looked down on these performers and considered them sinners and began their own plays with priests acting and performing stories from the Bible for the many who could not read the holy book.

Circus
During the mid-nineteenth century there were hundreds of circuses in Britain. Horse-riding tricks were the main attraction but there were also many other acts on offer. So popular were these displays that theatres hosted circus acts such as jugglers and air stunts. High-wire acts were performed in theatres around the crowds sitting in the stalls. Circuses were a hard business, constantly being on tour with no permanent home and often away from the family. During the eighteenth century, they toured even the smallest towns and villages. So popular was the appeal of the circus that many travelled across Europe and the USA, many making use of the new railways. One reason for the popularity of the circus was that the performers would travel to the audiences making the circus accessible to all.

Philip Astley created the first circus in London around 1768. After being discharged from serving in the Seven Years' War he settled in London where he taught at his riding school and performed riding feats and stunts. It wasn't long before he realised that he could make more money performing than teaching and started to search for other acts to accompany him including fire eaters and clowns.

Today there are many world-famous circus performers from all corners of the globe which include those performing high-wire acts, fire performers, horses and dancers and the ever popular clowns. It is thought that clowns began life in the Middle Ages as jesters and fools. By making fun of society these jolly chaps could often make the feelings of the public known and they sometimes helped with political ideas and change. Their costume has always been bright and colourful, green, yellow and red being the dominant colours, with hooded caps adorned with bells.

Entertaining on the street or in the courts, they performed a variety of skills such as magic, juggling and storytelling. Clowns have also been portrayed through history as Harlequin and his patchwork costume and Pierrot who was one of the earliest to use white make-up. They were more romantic than comic and have always added a loveable element to the circus ring although some think there they are rather sinister and certainly not always as jolly and fun-filled as they look – there have even been reports of ghost clowns . . . more later!

Ventriloquism
It is difficult to imagine that this strange variety act has roots dating back to the sixth century. Legend says that the act began as a way to communicate with the dead and had sinister and dark origins. Ventriloquism was greatly frowned upon

Pierrots.

by the Church and it wasn't until the nineteenth century that it was looked on merely as an act and entertainment. Since the 1940s this form of entertainment has celebrity status; it is a skill. A conversation is had between the doll and the ventriloquist who performs both voices. The skill is performed when the dummy speaks convincingly but the artist's mouth is not seen to move. We are tricked into believing that the dummy is speaking! And lots of us are! There are many spooky stories associated with this art about which I will tell you later.

3

SEAFORD

Seaford is a delightful, tranquil and charming coastal town close to Eastbourne and Brighton. During the Middle Ages it was one of the main ports in the area but declined at the hands of the pirates and the French in the 1300-1400s. The French even burned down the town several times.

Locals were known as being quite evil at times and they would lure a ship into the harbour by a false light knowing that the ship would run aground on the rocks in the harbour area if misguided. Once the ship had run aground it would be looted by the locals. Sea monsters were also said to lurk off the shores of Seaford but these tales may well have been told by local smugglers not wanting others to find their stash of illicit goods hidden close to the shores of the town.

Seaford was rescued in the nineteenth century when the railway finally arrived in the town connecting it to Lewes and London. This brought with it all the fortunes of becoming a small seaside resort and the construction of more houses to accommodate visitors. Businesses thrived and Seaford became known as a genteel and quiet resort rather than larger resorts such as nearby Brighton and Eastbourne.

The town is home to the westernmost Martello Tower built in the late nineteenth century as one of the sea defences along the South East coast; others can be found at Eastbourne and Camber. These delightful towers are situated on the beach and the one at Seaford is now the local history museum. During the Second World War there were large military camps in the town.

Seaford has earned itself a grand place in education in England and between 1900 and 1950 was one of the renowned school towns in the country.

The much-loved Barn Theatre in Saxon Lane opened in 1927 and was purchased by the Seaford Operatic Society in 1980. The flint barn dates back to the eighteenth century. Much love, time and hard work has been put in by loyal supporters of the theatre and it is a vital part of the community.

A visit to the seaside would not be complete without a hunt along the shoreline for shells and many people take them home as mementos of their visit to the coast.

Cowry shells have long been worn in cultures who believed that they represented fertility. They were also used in Chinese burial rituals: when an emperor died and was buried in ancient China, he would have had many cowry shells placed in his mouth.

Sea shells come in all shapes and sizes, the smallest being as small as a grain of rice and known as a clam. The largest is also a member of the clam family and found in the seas of the Pacific Ocean. The Aztecs used large conch shells as trumpets and so did Neptune's trumpeters to summon their king.

It is possible to find out about the creature that lived in a shell by looking closely at it. A low wide shell indicates that the creature had many predators and lived in an area with strong waves. A thinner conical shell shows that the creature would have come from much calmer waters. Shells and shellfish have played an important role in medicine; cockle clam was said to be good for the heart and pearls ground into a powder and mixed with herbs were once used to help stomach disorders.

Ancient Greeks and Romans depicted shell symbols for prosperity – maybe that is why we are so eager to have shell-shaped and inspired objects in our homes today. During the seventeenth century shell collecting and decoration was a hobby of the aristocracy and this was an era that inspired shell architecture and designs. In the nineteenth century women would collect tiny shells to design intricate patterns and detailing behind glass.

Looking around today much has been influenced by the sea and sea creatures such as home ware and decoration, jewellery and in particular bathroom designs. There is and always has been a magical mythical sense attached to the sea and the creatures from the deep.

I remember as a child visiting Seaford and the lovely beach there, searching for shells and other sea creatures along the shore with my school friends.

A box of seashells and other items dating to the 1930s were discovered at the Barn Theatre at Seaford – they had been packed away and probably forgotten about. The beautiful large shells had something rather enchanting about them – whenever the shells were moved, sounds of the sea where heard from within them. This even happened when the sea at Seaford was very still and calm like a millpond. Of course the sea can be heard in any shell but the strange thing about these shells was that the sounds were audible from quite a distance. It was as though the shells were haunted by their past, from where they had originated. It was decided to return them to the beach as that is where they really belonged.

4

ST LEONARDS

The Royal Concert Hall and Opera House in Warrior Gardens was very popular during the years 1878-1897. It had a seating capacity of 1,400 and was a venue for concerts and theatre performances. Later it was turned into the Elite Cinema. Sadly the building was destroyed by bombing in 1942. A strange phenomenon concerning spontaneous human combustion is linked with this building.

Spontaneous human combustion has mystified and intrigued many since time began. How the human body can suddenly burst into flames and burn until nothing is left except the victim's footwear is the stuff nightmares are made from. It is a subject which has caused great controversy. There any many so-called explanations and theories for this bizarre activity, some with supported scientific details and others a little more sinister!

One such theory is called the wick effect where the victim's clothing soaks up melted human fat and acts as a wick would on a candle.

Another possible cause is the static flash-fire theory in which there is a build up of static electricity in the body of the victim at such a highly dangerous level that a spark ignites the body. There is also the supernatural chain of thought which says that those who have evil tendencies and perhaps worship the devil will burn on the earth as the devil did in hell.

Whatever way you choose to look at this strange phenomenon it is highly intriguing. People around the world claim to have survived bursting into flames for no apparent reason; others have been less fortunate, including Charles Barnaby, an illusionist in the 1800s in the Hastings area who would appear at the concert halls in Warrior Gardens in his new and daring acts, loving to shock and surprise. However Charles's audience were not prepared for what happened during one such performance that went tragically wrong. He suddenly burst into flames and burnt to death on the stage in front of hundreds of naive on-lookers who thought this was part of the act. It is said that people only knew something was wrong when the smell of burning flesh became overpowering, by which time it was far too late to save poor Charles. It was said that nothing like this had ever been witnessed before. Everyone assumed that Mr Barnaby was just performing one of his crazy acts but little did they know that he was a victim of spontaneous human combustion.

This theatre always had a strange feeling in it after his death and sometimes the strange smell of burning flesh would linger. Some felt that it was a good thing that the building was bombed and destroyed in the war, however some still report a strange smell in the area today! Could this be the ghost of Charles still lingering on?

St Leonards Pier Ballroom
St Leonards Pier was opened in 1891 in the new resort of Burton St Leonards. It was positioned directly across the road from the Royal Victoria Hotel and became a direct rival to the pier at Hastings further along the coast. During the Second World War the pier was greatly reduced in size to minimise the risk of invasion; after the war it never really came to life again and was removed in 1951.

During the pier's heyday there was a magnificent ballroom at one end. Visitors from the cities could dance out at sea to the tunes of the time performed by bands and orchestras; it was *the* place to be seen and sport the fashions of the era. Many lavish and grand events were held there and the two piers vied to host the grandest show. The sound of the orchestra playing was often so loud that it could be heard for miles inland.

It was a sad event in the 1950s when it was decided to remove the pier from the shoreline. Today all that remains of the grand structure is a plaque on the promenade at the spot where the pier existed.

However all is not lost. Sometimes people have reported hearing an orchestra playing as they have walked along this section of the promenade, the music vivid yet at the same time dreamlike. This only happens during the night when people are on their own, walking their dogs or just taking a stroll. It is said that the music is the sound of yesteryear lingering on, beautiful ghostly music from the grand parties and balls which were held on the pier all those many moons ago. Such happy times were had at St Leonards Pier that it is not surprising that some spirits have chosen to linger on.

5

RYE

Some eleven miles from the busy seaside town of Hastings across the marshes lies the enchanting medieval town of Rye. Perched high on a hill it is easy to see how it was once surrounded by the sea giving the town great defences against invaders. Rye has a long maritime history being one of the Cinque Ports, and during the eighteenth century it was one of the main centres for smuggling. Secret passageways and tunnels still exist under the quaint streets and cottages. It is hard to imagine such illicit goings-on could have happened in this chocolate-box town which has always had connections as a prime trading port. Take the time to explore this medieval gem and you will find a maze of streets and snickleways (many leading to dead ends).

Rye has boasted a fruitful market for centuries and hosts potteries, antique shops and superb tea rooms. It was the home of authors Henry James and E.F. Benson. Around 1380 four magnificent gates and a wall were built around the town although little still exists. Rye is unique and it feels as though you have stepped back in time when exploring the cobbled streets and hidden treasures.

Mermaid Street is the town's most famous street with the Mermaid Inn offering a welcome rest to weary travellers. It is said that the Hawkhurst Gang, an evil and vicious band of smugglers, used to meet here in the mid-1700s to talk over their plans and drink into the small hours. Locals would fear to enter the inn when the Gang was in town!

Legend says that the bar area at the Mermaid is haunted by a victim of the Hawkhurst Gang, who returns now and again in the hope of meeting up with his murderers for revenge. Drink here if you dare!

Phantom Freak Show at the Horse and Groom Inn
The Horse and Groom Inn was once a theatre but was demolished in 1846. Travelling theatres and freak shows took place in Rye whereas some of the

larger towns and resorts did not welcome them. Freak shows put 'on show' anyone who was different to the way nature intended such as outcasts of normal society and people who were not accepted in everyday life. Here they would find a home and friends who became more like family; they were also paid well for looking and being abnormal.

The performing acts were designed to shock and many did this in great style with faint-hearted ladies running from the show. Freak shows were popular between 1840 and 1890 and mainly exhibited humans but some showed animals, such as the two-headed cow. As developments in medicine occurred it was realised that these freaks of nature as they had once been looked upon, were people with medical conditions and disabilities; they failed to shock the public anymore. This brought with it the death of such shows.

The freak shows which exist today have acts which are self-constructed and not medically achieved. Heavily tattooed and pierced bodies are on display – gone are the times of the mutilated human form and it is now more of an art show than a horror show.

Deformed humans were displayed at the freak show in Rye and the spirits and sites of these poor dear souls have chosen to linger on here. Even though the theatre is long gone, its ghosts still haunt the area today. The human exhibits of the time were very shy and did not like to be out of their group where they felt safe and secure. Many were looked after by the other members of the show and one gentleman in particular was totally reliant and dependent on his sister. His name was Bernie 'the body' Castleford and his sister's name was Franny. They were devoted to each other, both having disabilities and deformities setting them outside of normal life. Franny was dumb and deaf and her brother Bernie had been born with no limbs. They had earned good money by joining the touring theatre but had never been to the town of Rye before and this was their first visit. Bernie and Franny were always together – where you saw one of them the other was always close by, they were inseparable.

However one fateful day something awful happened and the pair lost each other in the crowds which had gathered to see them. Some local lads thinking it would be funny to push Bernie in his wheeled cart into the nearby river to see if he could swim took him from his sister and turned him into the waters. Bernie screamed for Franny and all the young lads could do was run away and laugh at what they had done. Poor Bernie drowned very rapidly in the waters at Rye, never to see his sister again. Fanny was distraught and the whole show hunted high and low for Bernie but to no avail. The show was stopped and the townspeople eventually came forward and told of what had happened. The culprits were thrown in jail for a long time for murdering poor Bernie but as for Franny, the whole business sent her crazy and she was found hanging from a tree in St Mary's churchyard, Rye.

Bernie haunts the area; blood-chilling cries for help can be heard and have been reported by walkers who have been down by the river's edge but no one has ever seen where the cries are coming from. They are said to be the final cries of poor Bernie before he drowned. Some people have also reported seeing a figure hanging from a tree in the graveyard but by the time they have reached the tree the figure is nowhere to be seen.

6

LEWES

Lewes lies approximately nine miles inland from the coastal town of Eastbourne and is approached along a long road sweeping across the Lewes Downs.

The Long Man of Wilmington (giant man cut into the downland turf of Windover Hill around ten miles to the east of Lewes) looks down on passers-by wishing them a safe and pleasant journey as he has done for years. Legend says that he is the guardian of the South Downs and his presence has mystified many for centuries. Where did he come from? No one actually knows which makes him all that more intriguing. Some say that he was created and drawn into the hillside by the local monks between the eleventh and fifteenth centuries; others say that he is prehistoric, or that perhaps he was a fertility symbol or an ancient warrior but whoever he was, he is a welcome sight to many and certainly draws the crowds. To me he is standing at the gates to somewhere which one day we will all discover!

Lewes today is a delightful town of significant importance with the headquarters of several local authorities being stationed here. It is also a thriving commercial centre, littered with curiosity and antique shops and markets and is ideal for anyone with magpie tendencies!

It is believed that the name of the town dates back to Saxon times as *Lewes* is Old English for hills. It is thought the town was founded in the sixth century. By the tenth century it was an important centre, having two mints and weekly markets. The Priory of St Pancras was established in Lewes; sadly all that remains today of this beautiful building are the imposing ruins as it was destroyed in 1538. The Franciscan friars were similar to monks but instead of keeping themselves to themselves they actually took their preaching into the world and were called the Grey Friars from the colour of their habits. In the Middle Ages Lewes was a very important port with large exports of much grain and wood. The plague took its toll on the inhabitants in 1538 when many lives were lost.

In 1845 the Lewes/Brighton railway was opened and this brought many people to the town, increasing trade. However this ended the port of Lewes, travel and transport by rail being quicker and more accessible. It was during the building of the railway that the tombs of the founder of the priory were discovered – these were the tombs of William and his wife Gundrada.

Dark Shadows at Lewes Castle

Another stunning focal point of Lewes is the motte and bailey castle set at the top of the town and in perfect condition – it looks as though it was built yesterday! There is an amazing view of the town and beyond from the castle. Interestingly the castle gardens are used during the summer months as an outdoor theatre and I can't think of a more enchanting backdrop to any production. It is said to be haunted by a hooded cloaked figure who lurks and hides in the shadows. Maybe he is one of the smugglers who hid illicit goods in the castle and was publicly executed for this crime. He certainly acts as though he is up to no good and people who have seen him say that he acts in a shifty way, as if he is worried about being followed.

Gaslight arrived in Lewes in 1822 and electricity in 1901. The grand town hall was built in 1893 and the Victoria Hospital in 1910. Lewes has continued to be a very prosperous market town ever since and is a delight to explore.

Friendly Ghost at Glyndebourne

Glyndebourne is famous for its outstanding operatic performances but have you ever wondered about the origins and history of opera? The word opera actually means 'to work' in Italian. The first opera, *Dafne*, was written by Jacopo Peri in around 1597. The first audiences were in the courts but by 1637 there were publicly attended operas for which tickets were sold. Opera has come a long way since it first started and now many towns and countries have operatic societies. Today opera has something to offer to everyone with operas set in modern-day life as well as around historical events.

In the early days of opera a living could not really be made by an operatic singer as performances were irregular, however today things are very different with professional operatic singers and performers earning very significant amounts and making a lifelong career in this field of work. The popularity of opera has changed; once seen as something for the older generation, today it attracts the young and is taught in colleges.

A few miles into the South Downs countryside is Glyndebourne House. The age of the building is unknown but parts are said to date back to the 1600s. Since 1934 it has opened its doors to music and opera festivals on a grand scale for which it is world famous. It began with the owner holding regular music events in the house which further developed when he was on honeymoon and attended the Salzburg Festival. It was that trip which inspired John Christie to bring professional opera to the house and make Glyndebourne alive. He wanted to bring the beauty and passion of the opera to the south coast.

Above and below: Glyndebourne Opera House has a friendly ghost of a small child in old-fashioned clothing. (© Jonny White)

Over the years much has changed at the old house and the auditorium has been adapted to accommodate the growing numbers of opera lovers. During the Second World War, it was used to house evacuees from east London. The house today is very much different to the one of yesteryear but the modern and ancient architecture compliment each other bringing together an elegant award-winning building. Many thought that Glyndebourne with its new ideas and modern approach would be short lived. Little did they know of the huge international success that Glyndebourne would have on. Its name is known and respected the world over.

Glyndebourne is said to have had spooky goings-on from when the house was first built. Even then it was a fine and elegant example of architecture and had magnificent gardens and an ornate and decorative well. The well, however, had a tragic tale connected to it which is said to be the cause of the haunting. In this period there was a cook working in the house who had a young daughter who would often come up to the house and sit in the gardens when her mother was working. However one day the young girl decided to explore a little further and found the well. Intrigued and curious she leaned into the darkness and unfortunately leant a little too far and fell in. It was very deep and no one heard her screams as she fell to her death – she was later found when a full search of the estate was carried out. Over the years some visitors have mentioned seeing a young girl sitting in the gardens of the house wearing an old dress of ancient style and with her hair in braids. She looks as though she has stepped out of a history book. No one has ever felt afraid of this little spirit but they are curious as to who she was.

7

HAILSHAM

Hailsham is one of the main towns in the Wealden District of East Sussex and is deeply rooted in agriculture. In 1252 King Henry VIII granted a charter giving Hailsham a market; a cattle market is still regularly held in the town. Rope-making was also carried out and Hailsham became a major supplier of the rope that was used in public hanging executions all over the country!

In 1849 the railway came to Hailsham and the Cuckoo Line ran to Tunbridge Wells and Polegate – sadly it stopped running in the 1960s.

The town centre has seen many of its old public houses close including the Cow, the Markey House and the Fox (many of the names keeping the traditional rural link to the town alive). The George and the Grenadier pubs are still located in the area known as the Triangle.

The Corn Exchange has an interesting past with films being shown in the 1900s before Hailsham Pavilion was built in the early 1920s. The Corn Exchange is rumoured to be haunted by a film shown here which caused such controversy that it was banned. It featured ladies of the period scantily clad and was considered far too risqué for the quiet and well-meaning country folk – it was thought to have been better directed to the resorts of Brighton and Eastbourne and the City of London. The gentleman responsible for showing this film was sacked from his work and his bag packed for him by his landlady who threw him out into the street. He was homeless with no job. To add to his woes as he walked through the countryside on the edge of Hailsham he was set upon by thieves who stole what little money and possessions he had on him. The poor chap just couldn't take any more and sat by the roadside wondering what to do. No one really knows what happened to him after that but some say that he died of a heart attack as he could not take any more stress in his life. Others say that he continued wandering the streets and roads and eventually made his way back to Hailsham where he lived a very strange life in the attic of the Corn Exchange until his dying day. He only ventured out after dark and lived off food that was thrown away from by shops and

Above and below: Ornate carvings at Hailsham Pavilion.

cafes. Today people are reminded of him by the sounds of footsteps at the Corn Exchange when there is nobody around. No one seems afraid of him and some quite like to think he has chosen to return here.

Another building with an interesting past is Hailsham Pavilion. Built in 1921 as a purpose-built picture palace it caused much upset in the community with many fearing the new and modern approach to showing films. Its interior was painted yellow and pink and extensive gold leaf was used on its ornate wall décor. It had solid-wood panelling carved with faces and flowers. Beautiful plaster figures of children carrying flowers, bread and fish were carved in the plaster work, the doors and walls were French polished and rich velvet curtains hung in front of the large. Officially a Grade II Listed property it is also inside Hailsham's conservation area. Inside and out the building has a grandiose feel and has been compared to architecture in London and Paris. The auditorium measures 2,400sq ft and at the time when it was originally built it seated an audience of 397.

It was used during times of war for troops stationed in the area. Sadly it closed as a cinema in 1965 and stood empty until 1967 when it opened as a popular bingo club. The club lasted until 1985 when it was sold once again and stood empty for several years, badly neglected with damp, vandals and pigeons taking over at every opportunity. Over the years that followed the people of Hailsham were quite passionate about the pavilion and its outcome and they raised funds to restore it into a unique building, showing films in a wonderful setting.

A ghostly tale connected to the pavilion dates back to when it was a bingo hall and I was told this tale by someone who worked there as a bingo caller. He was often in the building on this own although he felt as though there was someone or something else in there with him. It would meddle with the bingo equipment as if playing with it – not in a spiteful way but more naughtyamischievous. He remembers also that at the time when the future of the pavilion was undecided the ghostly activity would increase as if the spirit was showing his feelings too. It was as though ghost was protesting in the only way he knew he would be heard. When the bingo hall closed the spooky goings-on continued and even when vandals broke in they didn't stay very long as they claimed that there was a strange feeling in the place. However all this ceased when the pavilion was refurbished to its former glory and reopened. It was as if some sort of guardian from the past was watching over the goings-on at the pavilion and was unhappy when it was not being used for its original purpose. Perhaps the ghost of the original team of architects is still watching over!

Tall, black, ghostly net huts on Hastings fishing beach. (© Jonny White)

Hastings Old town fishing beach – a heritage rich in folklore and superstition. (© Jonny White)

Hastings Old Town has a history of smuggling and many secret tunnels.

8

HASTINGS

Hastings Pier Theatre
Hastings Pier, modelled on Brighton's West Pier, was built in 1869 and took three years to complete, costing over £20,000. It had a pavilion at the sea end which was destroyed by fire in 1917. In the early 1900s small buildings were added which also housed various businesses and activities. A shooting gallery and slot machines were added in 1910 and later a bowling alley. During the 1930s Hastings Pier was one of *the* entertainment venues in the area where dancing, concerts, diving and boating trips took place.

The Second World War saw it reduced for fear of invasion; it was bomb damaged, but reopened in the late 1940s.

From famous stars to holiday makers, many people have enjoyed hapy times on Hastings Pier and it has become a landmark where people gravitate to on a warm summer's day. At the time of writing, the future of Hastings Pier is undecided and it is presently closed to the public. I hope that somehow it can be saved as piers are reminders of how tourism began and the impact of holiday resorts in history.

If you were to walk around on the pier you would find an attractive small arcade of boutique shops selling unique and enticing items. Recently workers who were decorating the shops told me that one evening they returned to their work late in the night to complete a project and commented on how amazed they were to see one of the shop units occupied by what looked to be a tea room. They said that the establishment was fully fitted out and looked just like one you would have found in Edwardian England – it was like a tea room from yesteryear.

What they found even more mystifying was that the next day when they returned to work, the tea room had vanished! They began to think that maybe they were going a little mad but several of them had witnessed it.

It wasn't until they spoke to their boss that they found out that this had been seen before. In the 1900s there was a wonderful tea room on that part of the pier which survived until the Second World War, a lovely addition to this tourist attraction.

The spirit of the tea room lingers on today – returning now and again to capture the hearts and minds of any who see it.

Music Hall, Public Hall Theatre, Robertson Street
During 1858 this building provided a venue for much variety of entertainment. Converted to showing films in the early 1900s, it was known as the Orion Cinema, finally closing in 1976. It was quite a well-known venue in Hastings, enjoyed by the locals. Many people who have worked here have witnessed strange goings-on such as projectionists losing film that was in front of them and projection machinery stopping for no reason and refusing to work again. A poltergeist was a frequent visitor and the staff became quite used to it. This whole area of the town is known for its ghostly goings-on and the men have refused to work in the car park on the seafront just round the corner. The spooky activity is put down to the sea and the pull it had in times gone by to people who were suffering from illnesses of the mind. It was believed that the sea air would cure them, but this seldom happened and many patients who were sent to Hastings to recover actually took their own lives by walking into the waters and not returning.

Linton Gardens
Set just a stone's throw away from the centre of Hastings in a residential area but hidden from many, is Linton Gardens, a delightful open space and sanctuary for locals and visitors alike. An open-air theatre opened in 1948 here and this provided a popular venue in the centre of beautiful gardens.

'Something Behind You' at the Odeon Cinema/Gaiety Theatre, Queens Road
The theatre was built as a private venue in 1882. It closed in 1932 and was converted into the cinema which we see today. It still remains a very central and impressive ornate building and towers over many in the centre of Hastings shopping area. Little has changed to the exterior of the building apart from the modern lights and it still retains much of its original grace and beauty.

The building is definitely not appreciated for its truly beautiful ornate façade, architecture and fascinating past. Built in the early 1880s opposite the town hall, it stands impressively on the corner of Albert Road and Queens Road nobly watching over life going on below.

There have been uncountable numbers of visitors over the decades and not all of them have left. At one point in the late 1970s patrons of the cinema would report a very peculiar occurrence but only if they sat in a particular seat in the auditorium. They reported that during the film they would be tapped on the shoulder and asked to be quiet – on turning round to reply to this strange request (as the person in question had not actually been talking) they would notice that no one was actually seated behind them. This strange unexplainable activity would happen again two or three time during the show.

Programme from the Gaiety Theatre. (© Hastings Library)

Gaiety Theatre, now the Odeon Cinema, Hastings. (© Hastings Library)

This story goes back to when the building was a theatre and a notorious gentleman never liked anyone to sit in front of him during a show. He considered all people to be unclean and he did not want contact with anyone. He would make out that the person in front of him was disturbing his enjoyment of the show by talking (even when they weren't) and would tap them on the shoulder and ask them to be quiet. He would repeat this until they got up and found another seat. When they did eventually move he would laugh hysterically. During the late 1970s and early 1980s people reported a feeling of someone tapping them on the shoulder during the film and asking them to be quiet – however when they turned round no one was there! Although today this strange phenomena seems to have died down, beware of who is sitting behind you!

Witchcraft and Sacrifice at the Hare and Hounds Inn Theatre, Old London Road, Ore

Built before 1800, the theatre provided a venue on the edge of the town but sadly burnt down in 1867.

It was built close to the site of the entrance to the town and also the site of the gallows for the town. This area is still said to have the spirits of the dead running around. Very close to the east hill where much witch craft has been practiced, this site could be one of the most haunted areas in the town. Dark-cloaked figures have been reported walking through walls of this old inn and also the heady smell of jasmine can be smelt now and again.

Legends say that at the time when this was a popular venue a young lady would often sing here and entertain the people of the area however it is also said that she was involved in the dark arts and would worship the devil on the east and west hills of Hastings and also carry out sacrifices in the castle grounds. She was very beautiful and men were bewitched by her and fell under her spell – which was all part of her plan. For she would then lure them to the castle where she would drug them with her spells and potions and then sacrifice them to Satan! She was known for the pure jasmine oil perfume she wore and this smell drifts through the Hare and Hounds quite frequently. Men are very wary when this heady scent is in the air as to which females they choose to speak to . . . just in case she is a witch!

The Music Hall Singer at the Cinema De Luxe

Also known as the Empire Theatre and Royal Marine Palace of Varieties, this had ornate baroque style plaster decoration, magnificent balconies and boxes. It became the Royal Cinema in 1910, the Cinema De Luxe in 1912 and later in the 1960s was altered into a bingo hall.

It is easy to imagine how this magnificent building was once the heart of Hastings society. People came from all around to watch and listen to the varieties performed here including short plays, recitals and singing. However for a young lady from a wealthy background, the music hall was not the place to be seen. Being employed in this type of work gave the wrong impression about your family and

The Cinema De Luxe, Hastings, originally known as the Palace of Varieties.

it was certainly frowned upon if you were a young lady who hoped to marry one day.

The music hall had one young songstress who sang under the name of Elaina, the daughter of a wealthy local family in Hastings Old Town, yet she led a double life. She loved her evenings singing on the stage but knew that if her parents found out what she was doing they would be upset and would demand she stopped singing. Singing meant the world to Elaina and it would break her heart to ever have to stop, but she also felt bad lying to her parents in this way. When she was at the Palace of Varieties she told her parents that she was actually teaching young students to sing in their own homes. She always took with her a change of clothes so that at the last minute she could change into her more glamorous wear with her feather boa and her velvet gowns – the look for which she was known.

Elaina thought that she had kept her secret safe, however the old town was a very small place and everyone knew everyone else and what they did, good and bad! It did not take long for the news of his daughter's evening employment to get back to her father. On hearing the news her parents did not know what to think, all they knew was that it would bring shame to the family name and they knew that there was only one thing to be done, to bring an end to their daughter's scandalous lifestyle.

Palace of Varieties, Hastings. (© Hastings Library)

They decided that they would approach their daughter after they had seen her perform and so they bought tickets and took their seats at the Palace of Varieties. They listened in shock and horror as their daughter sang to her adoring fans. At the end of the performance they stood up and made themselves known and told how deceitful their daughter her been, demanding that she came home immediately with them and forbidding her to sing there again.

Elaina did not want to leave the theatre, she was happier there than anywhere else. She had never felt true love and to have the crowds calling her name was magic. The theatre brought her alive and she wanted to stay there forever even if it meant that she would never see her parents again. She was so distraught that

Palace of Varieties, Hastings. (© Hastings Library)

she committed suicide and was found hanging in her dressing room with a note which read, 'I want to be happy for ever and this is the only way'.

Elaina got her wish and her spirit has never really left the building. Her golden voice is heard by staff and visitors alike. The ghostly figure of a young woman dressed in long, rich, luxurious gowns and feather boa, with a spring in her step and singing a tune is often seen strolling down George Street. She disappears into the back of a house and it can only be one person, Elaina.

Alexandra Park's Magical Invisible Band
A stroll in Alexandra Park was not complete on a sunny afternoon without stopping at the bandstand and listening to the tunes played by the local band. Many open-air concerts were performed in the park and the bands of yesteryear are still heard today even when they are not playing music in the area. Some people have reported being drawn to the park on hearing music from nearby houses only to be quite confused on finding no band playing there!

Smugglers Revenge, The Bourne Hall Theatre
Hastings Old Town in the early 1800s was a place of great change. The new resort town of Hastings further along the coast was attracting people away from the old quarter in favour of newer and better prospects. Families were moving away and businesses were suffering resulting in new venues to entice people to stay. Drinking establishments offered new drinks, cafes opened up and it was realised that something had to change if people were to stay. One such addition to the old town was the

Alexandra Park.

building of a new theatre – close to the sea and yet right in the heart of the old town on the Bourne Road.

Built in 1825 at a cost of £2,500, it was not very successful and was forced to close in 1833 probably due to the rather risqué and brassy performers and acts that appeared here. Some say it was doomed before it started with the Church being severely against it and so it was sold to the Methodists in 1834. In more recent times the Bourne Street Theatre has been used for its original purpose and shows and performances for the community of the old town are held here – with great success. During the early part of its life, the goings-on at the theatre were deeply frowned upon by the Church and those who moved in religious circles. Exotic dancing girls, comedians of a rather dubious nature and acts exposing hilarity in the religion of the day brought such disapproval.

The Church blamed the little theatre for much of the bad behaviour and crime in the old town (although this was more of a poor excuse than actual fact). It said that the crude and vulgar goings-on were not what the old town folk were used to and that they were being led astray by such acts.

No one was forcing the public to go to the theatre and the Church was not amused that so many parishioners had turned away from its establishment in favour

Above and below: The Bourne Hall Theatre, Hastings.

of a more light-hearted approach to life at the theatre. Within a year of it opening it was closed and reformed into a Methodist church.

Today it is a small, popular art venue putting on music and art exhibitions which have proved to be extremely popular. However spirits of yesteryear have chosen to linger on sometimes making a nuisance of themselves when a show or other attraction is staged which may have caused a stir to the Church long ago. It is as though the spirits are still disapproving and will play around with lighting, water and any method in which they can make themselves heard. One local person reported how, during an evening performance by a local singer and group, the lighting kept flickering, little by little to begin with and nothing was really thought of it until the singer got up on stage and started their show. Something was making the lights angry and all of a sudden they went out and refused to come back on. It is said that the lead vocalist was a descendant of one of the exotic dancers who performed there in 1834 of whom the Church so much disapproved. Do the spirits of the Church still want to make themselves heard?

Another connection with the town's smuggling past is another smuggling ghost – this time people have heard footsteps and the sound of someone dragging a heavy item along the ground. This ghostly activity has been heard in the vicinity of the Bourne and in particular near to the Bourne Street Theatre and the properties nearby. This spooky activity has a more sinister tale to it regarding the town's smuggling history.

The penalty for being caught as a smuggler was severe and executions commonly took place. The old town was a small, close-knit community; it has always been that way and probably always will be. Everyone knew each other, what they did, day after day and night after night and gossip was rife! Stories and rumours spread quickly and a smuggler had to be careful about how he carried out his daily activities and the secrecy that was involved.

Joseph Taylor was a Hastings fisherman in the 1550s. His family was large and poor and he often needed more money to feed them. He regularly carried out extra jobs for people, being well-known in the area. It wasn't long before one of the gangs of smugglers heard about him and approached him to ask if he would be available to help them with their work; the money was excellent and it would certainly help with his growing family; he was prepared for the risks he was taking. He told his oldest and closest friend under strict instructions that no one was to know. One night, however, his friend drank too much ale and it wasn't long before gossip was heard about his friend's extra income. Joseph could not risk this and knowing where the story had come from, he had to silence his friend and lay in wait for him one night when he was returning home along a dark passageway in the old town. Before the friend could defend himself, Joseph sprung upon him and slit his throat, dragging the body to the back of a disused building along the Bourne (where Bourne Hall now stands). It is the sounds of him dragging the corpse across the floor that now haunt the building – sounds for no apparent reason which have no pattern to them. Ghostly footsteps are also heard as though walking on an upstairs floor; the building had two storeys, now it only has one.

The White Rock Theatre, Hastings.

The Old Infirmary, White Rock Theatre
No visit to Hastings can be complete without a walk along the beautiful promenade. Several miles of seafront awaits the walker who can take in the bracing sea air and several beautiful landmarks including Hastings Pier. Directly opposite the pier is the imposing, colonial-style White Rock Theatre. Built on the site of an old psychiatric infirmary, the theatre is reputed to have several ghostly guests who have chosen to stay.

The Sussex Rooms are said to be the most haunted part of the theatre, maybe because this area was once the infirmary's mortuary. Several ghosts are said to tread the boards including a vivid appearance of what appears to be a nurse. She is said to be dressed in a starched, grey uniform with crisp white apron and hat. She is said to have a very stern and severe look on her face so much so that anyone who has seen her has been quite afraid and has not wanted to approach and ask her what she is doing. She is also said to be carrying something in her arms. She is actually carrying the baby girl born to one of the patients at the infirmary. The mother had a severe psychiatric illness and so the baby was taken away from her and adopted, however the mother was so distressed on hearing that her baby had been taken away from her that she threw herself into the sea and drowned. The mother's screams are heard to this day as she searches the hospital for her baby boy.

The hospital was built on this site opposite the sea as it was thought that the sea air would do the patients good and speed their recovery, however in the case of psychiatric patients it had the adverse effect and sent many to an even earlier grave.

The White Rock Theatre is well known in the area for the pantomimes that are performed here every festive season. One event which I fondly recall from my childhood was the annual outing to the local theatre (The White Rock) to see the festive pantomime. Part of the enjoyment was the atmosphere in the theatre – children with friends and family, laughter, happy faces, excited and awaiting the magic of the theatre to be transported to a magical land with fantasy characters from their favourite fairytales. Many characters were larger than life in over the top costumes – but this was all part of the act. Pantomime entertained and mesmerised thousands of children and still does to this day. Little has really changed. Up and down the country from large cities to villages some form of panto can be found around the festive period. From large star-studded productions to amateur dramatic groups everyone takes part and has fun. Pantomime can be traced back in history to the Middles Ages with its stories set around famous childhood fairytales, folklore and legends, such as the enchanting tales of the *Sleeping Beauty* or the family favourite of *Aladdin and the Lamp*.

The panto season runs for around four to eight weeks around December and often continues into February. A huge business has been built around the panto season with city theatres competing for the famous stars of the moment to tread their boards each year. Theatres and anyone involved in the leisure business hire extra support staff and hotels in the area benefit from the panto goers and the stars.

Although a pantomime often recalls a traditional fairytale it includes many modern-day elements and often controversial topics of the time, current affairs or famous people to keep up with the times. It must also include good and evil depicted in the characters of the villain and the fairy godmother. It is the combination of the traditional and the modern which keeps the panto as popular as it is and appealing to so many.

One word everyone associates with panto is 'slapstick', a word which originates from a wooden sword which transformed into a magic wand with the turn of the hand, making a flapping sound.

In 1800 a famous panto character was Grimaldi the pantomime clown, loved by all. His part on the stage was huge, and in some cases his popularity took over that of many other stars. Grimaldi appeared at theatres such as Drury Lane and Saddlers Wells in London and to have him in your panto was a sure success.

The panto dame is another larger than life character such as Widow Twankey in *Aladdin* or Dame Trott in *Jack and the Beanstalk* which were created from the music hall in the Victorian era. Often the dame's costume would be a in a style fashionable to that era, colours and designs that were popular or new risqué styles of the day. The ugly sisters were first played by women but this quickly changed into men playing the roles in the 1860s.

The principal boy is another traditional element of panto, however this character is played by a female and not a male as the name suggests. During the end of the nineteenth century it was very fashionable for ladies to take these roles such as

Aladdin or Dick Whittington. With more music halls on the rise this became a popular casting for women. It was also popular with the men. The Victorian era was very strict when it came to modesty – even the legs of a table were kept covered up, so women exposing their legs on stage was a treat for the men in society but was also considered very risqué for the time. Artistic licence allowed the ladies on the stage to wear such costumes whilst everyday dress was strict with no sign of leg or ankle!

Panto could never have become what it is without the many extras, such as the chorus of dancers and troupes often referred to as 'babes'. Famous troupes have included the Tiller Girls.

Children always remember the shouting and joining in with the antics of the show and shouting 'oh yes it is' and 'it's behind you'. Panto horses are also popular and remembered by all, with the two poor actors wearing the furry horse costume. Two in the front legs and two in the rear and the bottom! A much laughed-about part in the panto. The front end of the horse was once played by Charlie Chaplin and many stars of today have started off as one end of the panto horse or another!

The stage area of the White Rock Theatre is said to be haunted by a phantom panto horse from the early days of panto at the theatre. Two brothers played the role of the horse and tragedy struck when they fell to their deaths from the high stage. A ghostly panto horse has often been spotted by the audiences and also other members of panto casts. Sometimes audiences have been a little confused seeing two horses!

The Pretty Ghost and the Smuggler at the Stables Theatre, Old Town

Have you ever looked at a building and considered its history? Wondered what was there before, what the building would say if it could speak? Who has passed through its door? In my research I have always asked these questions as I am fascinated with the past and how events and people have played a part in a building's or place's history, be it positive or negative. Atmospheres from happy parties to barbaric torture and murder are shown in one way or another having being ingrained in the history of a building.

Walk to the top of the High Street in Hastings Old Town and you will find the Stables Theatre. The building there today is a combination of a 1956 building and the old stables for the troops who kept their horses there during the Napoleonic times. The Old Town Preservation Society saved the ancient stable block and preserved it as part of today's Stables Art Gallery and Theatre.

As many original parts of the building were saved and used in the new construction as possible and extensive work was carried out. Internally many of the original beams were used. Sir Ralph Richardson opened the theatre in 1959 by and since that time the venue has become second to none putting on professional performances and shows over the years. This little theatre has a vast reputation for the variety and quality of its performances which are often a sell out. Whether this is anything to do with the resident ghosts at the theatre is not known, but one of them is said to only appear on the opening night of a show if it is deemed to be a success. She is said to be the ghost of a young lady who lived in a large house across the street from the theatre, Old Hastings House. At this time it was the home of the Collier family and one of the town's most expensive houses, the equivalent of today's town council building. Elizabeth, the eldest daughter of the Collier family, fell in love with one of the soldiers who kept his horses at the stables. They would meet and go for long romantic walks on the east hill and it is said that they were to be married when he returned from war. Unfortunately Elizabeth was never to wed as her fiancé was tragically killed in battle. On hearing of his death, she was so distraught that she went to the east hill one evening to the spot where they would spend many hours talking to each other and threw herself from the cliffs to her death in the waters below. This area is now known as Lovers' Seat or Lovers' Leap.

Elizabeth's ghost has chosen to live on at the stables and many affectionately call her the 'pretty' ghost. She has been seen on the stage area by actors and audience who describe a tall, elegant looking lady wearing light-coloured floating gowns; she is a ghost people hope they will see!

Step back in time to somewhere between 1500 and 1800 and smuggling was big business in this area of the country. Deep old cellars and linked properties made ideal places for storing contraband which consisted of textiles from far away places, spices and herbs, teas with exotic aromas, spirits and other luxurious items.

East Sussex was ideal for smuggling with so many hidey-holes along the shoreline and intricate old streets and alleyways. In Hastings Old Town passageways leading off the High Street, George Street and All Saints Street were used by smugglers. Pubs, churches, cottages, indeed any building suitable to hide goods in were used including the local theatres.

Deep beneath the Stables Theatre and unknown to many, was said to be one of the most-used links by smugglers where large quantities of wine and spirits and teas were stored. This was a perfect location being close to churches and in between the east and the west hills with its complex maze of passageways and deep caves. During the smuggling times the Stables Theatre was the site of stable blocks used during times of war but left unused for long periods of time.

The ghost of a smuggler who was executed for his crimes is often said to be seen and heard rummaging about deep under the theatre. Believing he is part of the cast of a show or play, people are surprised when staff say that no characters resembling smugglers were taking part in the shows. Workmen have also been made aware of the presence of the smuggler and sometimes whilst working alone in the theatre have mentioned that they would leave tools in certain places, and return to where items had been left to find that they had disappeared. It is as though tools and equipment have just vanished into thin air! The items are always found, but in strange places. This particular smuggler ghost seems to have en eye for quality items and seems to be up to his old tricks – disguising his contraband!

Smuggled goods would have been brought ashore along Rock A Nore Road and up through the passageways and tunnels dug deep into the cliffs and hills. The tunnels emerged in such places as the Stag Inn on All Saints Street, only a stone's throw from the Stables Theatre.

The Stables Theatre, Hastings. Many underground passageways link the theatre with ancient inns and churches – many are haunted by old smugglers still looking for their hidden goods. (© Tina Lakin)

The Stables Theatre, Hastings. (© Tina Lakin)

The tunnels beneath the churchyard connecting to the Stables Theatre across the road are said to be haunted by smugglers who conceal their illicit goods in hide-holes – would you be brave enough to venture down there?

The tunnels beneath the churchyard connecting to the Stables Theatre across the road are said to be haunted by smugglers who conceal their illicit goods in hide-holes – would you be brave enough to venture down there?

The Stag Inn – mummified cats and rats are reminders of witchcraft in fifteenth-century Hastings.

Deep beneath this fireplace is the entrance to one of the many secret passageways used by the smugglers.

Hastings Old Town.

There are many ancient snickleways and twittens in the old town, where glimpses of the past still linger.

All Saints Church – many illicit goings-on took place here centuries ago.

9

EASTBOURNE

Eastbourne for many centuries was not much larger than a village. In 1232 permission was granted to hold markets in the town which increased incoming trade. In the sixteenth century it was described as a market town although it was still only was the size of a large village. However all was to change in the eighteenth century when sea air was considered healthy and many towns along the coasts of England were inundated with visitors flocking to take in the health-giving properties of the seaside.

Visitor attractions were built and with the railway coming to Eastbourne in 1849, the town's popularity increased; there was a vast improvement to its in 1851. Holidaymakers needed entertainment and theatres sprung up with the Devonshire Park being constructed in 1884 and the Congress in 1963.

Eastbourne was larger than Hastings yet smaller than Brighton, and was also more of a resort than the fishing town of Hastings which was looked down on by some. It was unique and offered something more upmarket and charming. It was almost like being in another country. It was also an ideal place to spend time recovering from illness. It featured up to four theatres, a pier, ballrooms, grand hotels, shops and glorious scenery to walk in including the cliff path area at Beachy Head to the west of the town.

The building of a pier began in the spring of 1866, finally opening in 1870. Its unique design allowed it to move in bad weather guarding against the harsh elements which this part of the coast can suffer. The pier itself has weathered well compared to neighbouring piers in Brighton and Hastings. It measures just over 300m and was originally built with two toll booths and numerous small kiosks dotted along its length. The 400-seat pavilion built in 1888 was replaced in 1899 with a 1,000-seat theatre. During the Second World War the pier's decking was replaced with machine-gun platforms.

In 1970 the theatre was tragically lost to fire but today the Atlantis Nightclub and bar is on its site.

The Congress Theatre, Eastbourne. (© Ben Herbert)

Devonshire Park Theatre, Eastbourne. (© Ben Herbert)

Above and opposite above: Devonshire Park Theatre, Eastbourne, where fascinating orbs and the ghost of a lady in blue have been seen.

Eastbourne Pier. A service man haunts the pier and his cigarette smoke is often seen.

Eastbourne Promenade. This popular and upmarket resort in Edwardian times saw a growth of the town's theatre.

Outskirts of Eastbourne, very popular with visitors from London – some have chosen to linger on where they were most happy.

Although today the pier is much modernised from the original it still offers all the charm and appearance of a pier and whenever I have visited it has always been popular and well enjoyed by all. It retains an air of nostalgia and grace and it is easy to imagine the elegant couples of yesteryear with their parasols and genteel attire strolling along the prom. You may think that somewhere as charming as Eastbourne would not be the place to find a ghost, however I have discovered many things which go bump in the night here!

Atlantis Nightclub on the pier is a popular venue for a night out and clubbers often step outside to get some sea air. Often they have thought they were alone but report seeing an army-type chap, smoking and leaning against the pier railings; sometimes he may acknowledge them before walking through the wall of the building.

Soldiers spent time here during the Second World War and their emotions would have been running high, being away from home and in a strange place not knowing anyone. They would have spent a few hours of fun in Eastbourne's bars and dance halls and even though it was wartime there would have still been some fond memories living on. So it is not surprising therefore that some of the wartime heroes have chosen to linger on here in a place where they were happy.

The Royal Hippodrome Theatre, Eastbourne

A little girl in old-fashioned dress (people have said either Victorian or Edwardian) has been seen on many occasions by actresses at the Royal Hippodrome in Eastbourne. The little girl appears in the dressing rooms when actresses are getting ready for their performances on stage. No one has ever felt afraid of this little figure; she actually brings a very calm feel to the nervous actresses backstage. She appears out of nowhere and is always seen seated in one of the large comfortable chairs in the dressing rooms. She has never been seen in any of the male dressing rooms or maybe they just do not see her.

All those who have been lucky enough to see her describe a young girl around ten to twelve years old with her hair in long curly spirals and wearing a rich, deep-blue velvet dress with lace panelling, frilly petticoats and patent-leather boots. She is well dressed and appears to come from a well-to-do family. She has never caused any trouble and is not a mischievous spirit but just quietly sits and watches whoever is in the room.

Her name is Emily Fogath and she is the daughter of a theatre manager who worked at the theatre when it first opened. She used to spend hours at her father's work, loving to mingle backstage with the glamorous stars of the day. She would try on their costumes and spray their perfumes. No one minded Emily being in the theatre; in fact they became used to seeing her around the place. However she had a weak heart and these were times when little was known about this condition. Sadly at the age of twelve Emily died after contracting bronchitis, which in her weak state she could not shake off.

She was a happy little girl and was greatly missed but her little spirit lingers on in the place where she spent so many happy hours.

Today Emily is still seen regularly and is a much loved ghost. Just goes to show that not all ghosts have to be scary!

Orbs at the Devonshire Park Theatre

Orbs have always fascinated people and whether you think of them as merely tricks of modern photography or spirits trying to communicate with us they continue to appear and enthral us all! Many do believe that these balls of light which appear in photography are indeed spirits or ghosts. Many people have felt comforted by the presence of an orb around them – linking them with people they have been close to who have passed away. Orbs have many identities appearing as balls of light in all shapes and sizes; even their colour can change from white (the most common colour) to shades of blue and green. They can be quite solitary or appear in numbers depending upon the situation.

Ancient Mayans said that some kind of spirit life is encountered as time goes by and we become closer to the spiritual world. The divide between ourselves and the spirit world is becoming less and less.

The medicine men of the Andes believe orbs to have existed for thousands of years and that they are found in areas of great spirituality. Whatever they are they cause great interest wherever they appear and I am sure this will always be so.

Much orb activity has been reported over the years at the Devonshire Park Theatre in Eastbourne. This beautiful Grade II Listed building dating to 1884 was vastly improved in 1903 and is a wonderful example of a Victorian theatre. It has elaborate decorative plasterwork and design and has a real feel of yesteryear – as though time has stood still. It can seat almost 1,000 people and its grandness adds to its appeal – it is no wonder that some spirits have chosen to stay around and make it their home.

Back in the early days of theatre the colour blue was expensive to create, whether for décor, material or lighting and, therefore, little used. Green and yellow were considered unlucky colours in the theatre world as it was said that the devil would disguise himself by wearing a hat or tie in these colours.

Orb activity has a long history at the Devonshire Park and several of them have been vivid blue in colour – there have also been sightings of several balls of bright blue which fade to pale blue and then white. This orb activity has been caught on photographs on various occasions over the years and there does not really seem to be any real pattern in their appearance.

The orbs are said to be the spirit of Annabella Charleston who sang at the theatre when it was first opened. She was renowned for her beautiful bright blue dresses, made from the finest-quality textiles from exotic lands. She was a popular performer and became famous for her dresses. It is said that she died of a broken heart when she found her husband with another woman. Annabella's spirit, however, lives on where she was most happy and surrounded by those who loved her.

10

BEXHILL

De La Warr Pavilion
Earl De La Warr, the Mayor of Bexhill, held a competition in the early 1920s to find someone to design a unique new building on the town's seafront which would attract tourists from around the world. He wanted somewhere where people could come to really appreciate a variety of arts and a building that would reflect the modernist times and attitude. Towns up and down the country were inundated with dark and airless Victorian architecture; now it was time to have a new design, and where better than in Bexhill.

It was to have huge windows which would reflect the sea and utilise natural light to the maximum; terraces were also a must so that people could enjoy music outside and take afternoon tea in the sunshine. Not only was this to be a breathtaking engineering achievement but also a whole new luxurious lifestyle would be created.

The idea which won the design was to be European and modern and with over 200 designs received it was the ingenious creation of Mendelssohn & Chermayetts which was breathtaking and awe inspiring. The design was one of sheer luxury, similar to travelling on an ocean liner heading for an exotic and far away place. It was designed with a dramatic central sweeping staircase and with so much light flowing through the building at all angles, a truly magical place was created.

The pavilion was opened in 1935 by the Duchess of York. It was a totally new experience for many in this sleepy little seaside town. Today the De La Warr Pavilion is an arts venue of international renown. Artists travel from all over the globe to perform and exhibit their creations at this beautiful building by the glittering sea.

Although it is a fairly modern building in comparison with some of the other theatres in this book it is not devoid of strange goings-on.

One fascinating tale is that of beautiful moving lights which linger off the shore directly behind the pavilion. Those who have witnessed them have described them as dancing fairy lights that seem to have a gentle feel about them. The most

Bexhill Old Town, where many secrets lie hidden. (© Ben Herbert)

Manor Barn Museum – elegant dresses of yesteryear are haunted by their past owners. (© Ben Herbert)

Bexhill Old Town – have you seen the phantom gypsy caravan?

Bexhill Old Town – have you seen the phantom gypsy caravan? Travelling theatres would frequently visit Bexhill.

A tragic ballerina haunts the de La Warr Theatre, and staff always know when she is about as ballet shoes appear in odd places. (© Ben Herbert)

De La Warr Pavilion, Bexhill, a magical creation by the sea.

common tale told about the lights is that they are the souls of mermaids who are attracted by the singing and music which feature at the pavilion and draws them to this magical place.

Spooky Shoes at the De La Warr Pavilion

Ballet has played a part in the history of the De La Warr with many international dancers performing here over the years.

The word ballet can be traced back to the Italian word meaning 'to dance'. Ballet has continued to grow and thrive over the centuries and has strong influences developing neoclassic, contemporary and post-structural ballet. One of the most elegant and beautiful dances ever to be performed, ballet has a history dating back to the fifteenth-century courts of the Italian Renaissance. It started as part of the form of fencing, a sport in which many of the movements are still used today.

Ballet is taught and performed the world over and although it may look very graceful and elegant and the movements appear smooth and unbroken, it has a very technical and precise discipline to it and the dancers are regimented.

Classical ballet is the most formal with has strict techniques and Russian influence; it is the basis for many other styles such as hip hop, modern and contemporary dance.

The attire is simple and has little changed over time:. pink, flesh or black tights and a leotard; a short wrap skirt can be worn by female dancers. The shoes are called flats and are made of supple leather or satin, sometimes fastened up the leg with ribbons. As a dancer develops they move on to the pointe shoes, enabling him or her to work on the end of their toes. However should a dancer wear these shoes before they are ready then numerous injuries and disabilities could be caused.

Although there are many regional variations in ballet, the principles remain the same. Folk and gypsy dance have classical ballet roots; neoclassical ballet has many roots in classical ballet but is less rigid. Contemporary ballet has classical and modern influences and is much less strict with more floor work.

When I was a little girl I was like thousands the world over and wanted to be a ballet dancer and nagged at my parents to allow me to go to ballet classes which I did from the age of five to around twelve. I often remember the graceful movements I was taught; it was as if they were drummed into me. One thing I adored more than anything were the wonderful ballet shoes, they were like magic shoes on my feet, so soft with long velvet ribbons; I adored them. Ballet shoes mould themselves to the feet of their owner and it is considered very unlucky to wear someone else's shoes.

This story could have come from the story at the De La Warr Pavilion. A dancer was performing here not long after it had opened but she had mislaid her shoes and so took those of a colleague to wear for a major performance. However as she danced on the stage she lost her footing and fell from the stage to her death. An unusual ghostly phenomenon is present at the pavilion and has mystified many who have worked here. Ballet shoes are sometimes found and left in strange places; no one can find an owner and then they disappear. Some believe that this is the ghost of the young dancer who tragically died at the pavilion years ago and is still making her presence known today.

Bell Inn Theatre, Old Town, Phantom Gypsy Caravan
Leaving the genteel retirement resort of Bexhill on Sea behind and walking inland slightly you will come to the old town area of Bexhill. Known for its beautiful Manor Gardens and littered with wonderful historic buildings and churches it really is a gem that is sometimes overlooked. Amongst the timber-framed cottages and shops and Regency-style properties, nestling in the heart of the old quarter, is the Bell Inn. For hundreds of years there has been an inn on this site providing a much-needed stopping point for weary travellers and coaches and horses en route to London and other towns. Prior to 1817 there were records of a theatre standing on the site that was favoured by touring companies. There was also entertainment at the Manor House during 1890-1911. I have heard many enchanting tales of beautiful caravans arriving at the inn in early May as this was a favoured stopping point for many travelling theatres. People have told me that today in early May you can often catch a glimpse of the theatre arriving if you are lucky enough but you have to really believe in the gypsy folklore which brought this kind of theatre to life. Gentle, well-meaning folk would come to town for a short stay and bring with them their skills and acts to entertain local people and let them into their own magical worlds. Some frowned upon them but that could well have been just because they were afraid or did not understand their nomadic existence. Those who welcomed them were treated to a beautiful spiritual way of life that has lingered on in this area ever since. The people of the theatre brought with them their ways, handed down by their families through the ages, ancient traditions which didn't require bright lights and lots of money. They led a more simple life. They showed people the magic of flowers and herbs and how the moon could help in everyday life. The built fires, cooked wonderful food and performed puppet shows. Their enchanted music brought a whole new life to the area – it is no wonder that the spirits have chosen to return here every year.

Egerton Park Theatre
This was a semi-covered open-air theatre which closed in 1989; a bowls pavilion now stands on its site. The grandness of the theatre from past days can still be seen and the ghosts of a very elegant looking couple are often seen walking in the park area of Bexhill. Locals say that they are both well turned out and look as though they have stepped out of a history book. They disappear when they reach the area where the open-air theatre was built.

Royal Bijou Theatre, Town Hall Square
The Duel Cinema and Theatre was built in 1910 as part of the expanding and exciting new resort of Bexhill on Sea – sadly it was closed in 1954, however it retains a wonderful past connection with puppets!

Puppets are popular the world over – they are appealing in that they can they can convey emotions not usually expressed. Today's puppets can be very simple hand-puppet designs or complex and highly technical electronically manipulated designs.

Oscar Wilde once wrote: 'there are many advantages in puppets, they never argue, they have no crude views about art, and they have no private lives' – how very true especially when compared with actors and actresses of the day.

Puppets can be used for far more absurd and impossible ideas than human actors could ever act and have endless possibilities. The art goes back over 30,000 years ago and they have been used in cultures and societies to portray ideas and to communicate thoughts. Puppets made from clay have been found in the tombs of the ancient Egyptians who referred to them as 'small walking statues'.

The art goes back 400 years in India; China has had a puppetry heritage for the last 2,000 years with the 'theatre of lantern shadows'. In its Song Dynasty, puppets performed to all high classes in court, however at this time the art was still considered low-class entertainment in much of Europe.

Across Iran, Turkey and much of the Middle East, puppets have made an appearance in one form or another – when Yaruz Sultan Selim conquered Egypt in 1517 and saw its puppet theatre he took the idea back to the Ottoman Palace in Istanbul.

In ancient Greek the word puppet is *neuropasta* which translates into 'string pulling'. By the third century BC puppet plays were appearing at the Theatre of Dionysus at the Acropolis.

In Great Britain when we think of puppets we instantly think of Punch and Judy shows at the seaside as a child. However this show actually has its roots in sixteenth-century Italy as Punch and Judy shows originate from Italian mythology.

Today the growth and popularity has expanded with centres at the Little Angel Puppet Theatre in Islington, London, the Harlequin Puppet Theatre in Wales and several others.

Puppetry today reaches a far broader audience than ever before with the development of television, cinema and other media with its main forms being finger puppets, hand and glove puppets, rod puppets, marionettes, shadow puppets and human carnival or body puppets used in large parades.

Punch and Judy shows have always been a popular seaside entertainment; the easily transported theatres gave the puppeteer scope to travel around the country, appearing where he chose.

Punch and Judy husband and wife team, Bernade and Ewa Goldfriench from Prague travelled around the UK year after year always appearing at the Bijou Theatre in Bexhill to perform. They were a huge success with their audiences as they let children take a part in performing. They returned to Bexhill for many years until Bernade died and Ewa felt that she could just not go on without him. She gave the puppets and the theatre to the Bijou where they could continue entertaining children. However the Punch and Judy show declined over the years and the puppets and their mini theatre were stored in a back room.

In the 1940s some members of staff were clearing out the store room late one evening after work and came across the box of puppets and the mini theatre and decided to set it up. They were intrigued by the beautiful design of the puppets. Some of the staff carried on with their work whilst others played with the puppets, when, all of a sudden it was as though the puppets came to life and started performing on the little stage by themselves. Their colleagues assumed that one of their work mates was controlling them but when they looked behind the tent theatres no one was there and the puppets were still moving!

It is said that puppeteers and puppets develop a very strong bond as something of the puppeteer brings the puppet to life whether they are controlling them or not. Perhaps the puppets were haunted by their previous owners Ewa and Bernade.

Sadly the Bijou Theatre closed and what happened to Punch and Judy no one knows but maybe somewhere they still entertain the crowds!

Peacock Feather Folklore, York Hall Theatre, No. 126 Station Road

Built in 1895, the theatre was part of the York Hotel. At this time Bexhill was becoming popular and this was one of the first hotels built to accommodate the many visitors to this genteel and elegant resort by the sea. It was a popular hotel and it was not long before a theatre popped up to provide entertainment for guests and locals alike. This theatre had quite an active life for some forty years when it was converted into the Gaiety Cinema.

There is an eerie tale connected to the demise of the building which has links with 'peacock' feathers! In the theatre world, peacock feathers are strongly disliked by all actors and have associations with the ever-open eye and the evil eye. Those associated with the theatre believe that horrible misfortune will befall anyone given a peacock feather or one depicted in any form and that bad luck will befall a building that houses these brilliantly coloured feathers.

Legend says that a year before the theatre was turned into a cinema the manager was sent a bouquet which included peacock feathers. No one knows who sent them or where they came from – it was as if they appeared out of the blue. But no sooner had they appeared in the theatre foyer, bad things started happening. Guests started to dwindle in number at the York Hotel and this had a knock-on effect at the theatre and was associated with staff becoming ill. It was sold and converted into a cinema but suffered bomb damage in the Second World War. The building was derelict for years and was finally demolished and rebuilt as a garage in 1959. Some say that when the cinema was finally being demolished a single peacock feather was found in the ruined building.

The Lonely Pianist of Hove

To visit the upmarket resort of Hove just a few miles from Brighton, visitors would be forgiven for assuming that the town sprung up in the Georgian period, however it can be dated to the prehistoric age. In the hills surrounding the area, relics of long-gone times have been found and are proudly on display in Brighton Museum. Ever since the Roman period, grand dwellings have been built in this coastal town.

In 1910 Hove was a resort for the wealthy with shops in the Kings Road, five miles of promenade and beautiful residences facing out over elegant lawns and stretching down to the sea.

Along the grand promenade an open-air theatre was created providing genteel and classical entertainment. Musicians preferred Hove to the large resort of Brighton and enjoyed entertaining the audiences here as it was such an ideal spot. A talented musician, Edwards Mackenzie, is said to haunt the theatre area and it is the ghost of a young man torn apart by his girlfriend who ran away with the head pianist of a theatre in Brighton. He was a magical pianist but lacked the confidence of some who performed in Brighton. However he had a talent that could not be compared with anyone else and people travelled just to hear his beautiful playing. Edward was loved by all but the real love of his life – his girlfriend Geraldine Stone did not return his love in the way that he so wished for. She was not in love with him but loved another musician who worked in the Brighton theatres and was earning more money than she thought possible. He would buy her gifts and grand dresses and take her to elegant places to eat and drink. Edward could not live up to this standard as he earned very little at the open-air theatre. The final straw came for him one day when he was playing at Hove and he saw in his audience his girlfriend with her lover. He could not take any more and so when he had finished his session walked to Beachy Head and threw himself from the cliffs to his death below.

If you walk along the prom at Hove you will hear magical piano music. You will wonder where it is coming from – perhaps from the ghost of the poor pianist Edward Mackenzie?

11

BRIGHTON

Brighton has been settled since the Saxon period. In the humble beginnings it was mainly home to farmers and fishermen. During the 1300s there was an impressive daily fish market on the beach and a weekly market in the town which attracted people from the surrounding villages.

The first streets in Brighton were North, South, East and West Streets which still exist today; in the centre of the streets were allotments. The Lanes also begun here as pathways between the streets. Middle Street developed in 1500. Brighton was attacked by the French in 1514 who set fire to the town. Although the wooden, thatched roofed houses burned down very quickly they were easy to rebuild and by the late sixteenth century there were around 400 fishermen in the town. The fishing trade declined during the wars with the French and Dutch. Horrific storms destroyed much of the South East coast in the early eighteenth century including much of Brighton.

In 1750 Dr Russell wrote that bathing in seawater and breathing in the sea air was beneficial to health which brought the rich flocking to Brighton including the Prince of Wales in 1783. Hotels and guest houses, elegant squares, shops, cafes and theatres sprang up along the seafront. The fist theatre was erected in North Street in 1774. The first Brighton Pavilion was erected in 1787 in Grecian design, quite unlike the Indian-style palace rebuilt in 1815 and still in existence – it was used as a hospital during the First World War for Indian soldiers. The West Pier was built in 1866 followed by the Aquarium six years later and the Palace Pier in 1899; the first cinema arrived in 1909.

During the 1930s much of the slum area of Brighton was cleared and a new market at Circus Street built over the site. The Second World War damaged much of the town although The Lanes escaped undamaged.

Wandering around the town today you would not initially be aware of how many theatres and cinemas once graced this resort. During my research I was amazed at how many there were and how the people loved them. Sadly today many have changed use or are no longer in existence but their memories live on.

Open Area Street Theatre (Magic), The Lanes

From the Egyptians to the present day, people have dabbled in magic. Until the eighteenth century most magic was performed in the streets by magicians who needed little in the way of props. Magicians and magic, akin to witchcraft, has always been connected with an air of mystery.

The Lanes in Brighton is well known for its streets, full of character, lined with individual shops and bars and offering diversity to the high street. At one time The Lanes were slums with overcrowding and inadequate sewerage and water supplies. Many of the poor who lived here relied on begging to make a living. One such young lad was Jimmy Harbourne or 'Jimmy the Card' as he was known on the streets. Jimmy was loved by all who saw his magic – even the poorest of the poor would spend hours watching his show time and time again, and he didn't mind if they didn't have any money; he was just happy to be able to share his magic which had been passed down from his father and grandfather. Jimmy was a popular chap in The Lanes and many local people would rather stop and watch his act than pay to see a show in one of the large Brighton theatres. As Jimmy learned and performed new tricks he became more and more popular. It wasn't long before the magicians working at Brighton's large theatres heard about Jimmy and how popular he had become. Their work was suffering and magic acts were being axed from the theatres as ticket sales were low – many magicians were finding themselves with no bookings for which they blamed poor Jimmy and all decided that something must be done to stop this boy.

What happened to poor Jimmy will always be a mystery – perhaps a vanishing act similar to one of his tricks. But it is said that the magicians of the Brighton theatres murdered him in cold, jealous blood!

They set upon him one evening as he had just finished a show where he had been performing to a large group in The Lanes. They blindfolded him and dragged him along a dark and narrow alleyway between houses. Here they repeatedly stabbed him until he was well and truly dead. He was then disposed of by each member of the gang – it is said that parts of his body were used in their acts.

Jimmy's ghost still lingers on in The Lanes today. People have reported seeing a young lad in scruffy old-fashioned clothes performing card tricks to crowds of people and them simply fading into the air. His spirit is certainly here to stay – still entertaining the crowds as he always loved to.

And as for the rest of the magicians – gradually popularity of their magical acts depleted to be taken over by more modern acts and so their work well and truly dried up anyway!

Savoy Cinema (Cannon Cinema)

In the 1860s few houses had running water and the need for cleanliness brought about the building of public baths which could be visited by all. Not only were they places to wash but also for relaxation. Males and females were kept separate and in the male section, first and second-class citizens were divided too. Many public and Turkish baths opened around the turn of the twentieth century and were ornate in style, adding to the relaxing experience the bather was to enjoy. Beautiful mosaic floors, art nouveau-style tiling and elaborate glass windows all added to the luxurious experience away from the stress and strains of normal life. Bathers with medical conditions such as rheumatism could benefit from sea water without the harshness of the elements and prying eyes.

The first Turkish bath opened in Brighton in 1862 at No. 65 Western Road, Hove; it proved to be popular and was shortly followed by another at No. 57 Western Street, Brighton which was larger and more elaborate. A public bath stood on the site of where the Savoy Cinema (Cannon Cinema) stands today and this was in use until 1929 when it was demolished.

The Cannon Cinema has a fascinating past. The Savoy (as it was first known) had a seating capacity for 2,300 and boasted a unique underground car park. It had restaurants and cafes which made a trip to the cinema a night out. It became the ABC in 1963 and the Cannon in 1986.

Spooky goings-on here appear to have occurred for some time and people who have worked at the cinema over the years have become quite used to them.

One lady who used to clean here reported a very strange sound one evening when she was working alone. Knowing she was the only person in the building didn't frighten her as she quite liked the quietness and she was able to get on with her work. However what did scare her initially was the sound of water, not the kind of running water, more the kind of sound that you would hear at swimming baths, the echoing sound of the water in a building. On some occasions steam clouds would come from nowhere – the lady just thought she was imagining things or perhaps going a little mad until she learnt of the cinema's history and what had once existed on the site. It appears that the sounds and steam clouds went back to the public baths built on the old site.

Some visitors to the cinema have also reported feeling a strange clamminess and immense heat. Being one of the first of its kind in Brighton, the public baths would have had quite an impact on the town and would also have caused quite a stir within some circles. Maybe this is why a spirit has chosen to linger on today making sure that no one forgets the historical importance of what once was here in this part of Brighton.

The Orphan of the Alhambra Opera House and Music Hall, Kings Road

Built on the site of the old Whitehall stables behind No. 85 Kings Road, the Alhambra Opera House and Music Hall opened in 1888. Respectable shows featured here and it was host to many leading personalities during its twenty-four years. It was converted to film use in 1912 and the Odeon took over in 1936. The cinema closed in 1956 and was demolished 1963. Popular Brighton Centre now occupies the site and today hosts shows and concerts.

The life expectancy for young children and babies around the turn of the twentieth century was very poor. Babies and children often picked up disease and infections and it was quite common for them to be given a mixture of opium and alcohol to keep them quiet when crying from the pain.

Many things contributed to the death of the young: poor housing, severe poverty, lack of sanitation and medical care. In 1899 in the slums of Victorian England there were 509 infant deaths for every 1,000 children – appalling figures. Children contracted illnesses such as scarlet fever, whooping cough, TB, polio and tetanus. There were no vaccinations or medicine for the poor working classes of this era. The Brighton slums were a breeding place for disease and infection. With little or no mains facilities, waste was emptied into the streets which were the playgrounds of the young. It was no wonder that disease and infections spread through these areas rampantly taking hold of the weakest and the sickest. People who lived in the rural areas in Victorian England generally lived longer than those in the slums. It was primarily women who fell sick the quickest as it was tradition in Victorian homes to give the best food to the man of the house – in poor houses the women were often left with rotting food or nothing. In Brighton in 1865 the life expectancy was forty-six for the upper classes and only twenty-two for the working classes.

Children from poor families were forced out to work as soon as they could find paid employment, doing anything they could to bring a few pennies home. They risked life and limb in jobs that no adult would even consider doing. They were often sent under moving machinery in factories to collect garments, parts and so on, sometimes with horrendous consequences. Other children were sent to clean chimneys sometimes becoming stuck and suffocating. They also worked in the darkness of night and seldom saw the sunlight or felt it on their skin and that was one reason why rickets was such a problem. Little was known about medical conditions and certainly what little was known did not extend to the benefits of vitamins and minerals on the body and how essential it was for the body to maintain them, so no one would have thought that the sunshine could have cured a case of the rickets. Children who suffered from rickets were actually locked away in a dark hospital ward with little light or attention and they seldom came out of the institution alive.

Diarrhoea could kill a small child in forty-eight hours. Combined with the hot summer weather and poor sanitation there was no hope for some poor little mites who contracted a bad case of this stomach upset and many lives were sadly lost this way.

Measles was another significant killer in the UK in 1863 and 1874. Those who survived were sometimes left blind or deaf and they may as well have died as they were considered disabled and of little use to their families or the workplace. Crippled children were also frowned upon by Victorian society and the child and its family would be outcast from society, particularly those of the elite and upper classes.

Families who had significant and successful business interests were basically given a choice, your child or your business. Many families chose to continue successfully in business rather than to look after and care for their child. Compared to modern life today in the UK, this is relatively unheard of but in some cultures any child who has disease or a disability is looked down on as it is important for children to work from an early age. If they are unable to work they become a burden upon their siblings. In Victorian society children with an abnormality were looked on as freaks. Many poor families could not afford a funeral for a child and so parents would arrange with an undertaker to bury a deceased child in a grave with a stranger.

Children outcast by their family who had once loved and cared for them is a horrific thought. What kind of effect would this have had on the child, on their little minds? Put in an orphanage never to see their family again. None of the staff showed any love or affection to the children as they knew that they would not live for very long and considered it a waste of time. No proper medical staff were employed so children were basically left in a bed to die being given the bare minimum of food to keep them alive. There was little to stimulate or amuse them and no education at all. For many of the children who ended up in such places a little love and care was all that was really needed and they could then have gone on to live a perfectly normal life.

Society had given up on them – a very sad thought.

It is hardly surprising that the buildings that once housed the orphanages (although many have since been demolished) harbour the spirits of so many unhappy souls. One such orphanage was only a stone's throw from the high-society Alhambra Opera and Music Hall. The orphanage was so near that the children could hear the music and singing in their dorms. If they looked out of their windows they could often catch a glimpse of people going to the opera or music hall in their grand clothes. The children could only image and dream about what life in the theatre was like. One young lad Billy, who was crippled from ricket, fell in love with the music and planned to venture to the theatre as he so much wanted to be loved and have a family again. It took him a long time to get anywhere using his sticks to guide and support him; he was also weak through whooping cough from which he had once suffered. His clothes were ragged and he hadn't had a wash for weeks but he didn't care, and decided one night to leave the orphanage and find the theatre. He made his way along the dark corridors, down the main staircase and to the front door. The door itself was a challenge as it was so heavy to open but eventually Billy found himself out in the streets of Brighton. He was not afraid in any way; he saw other people like himself walking with sticks and wooden frames and one thing he knew for sure was that he would never ever return to that awful orphanage. Whatever it took he would not go back – even if it killed him.

It was very cold that night and as the rain came down Billy wished that he had a nice home to go to, but he was determined to find the theatre and to get inside the front door to the grand foyer. It wasn't long before he found the Alhambra and he just stood outside and looked up at the grand architecture and style of the opera house. People who were going into the opera house looked at him but he was used to that. Eventually when the performance had started and there were few people in the street Billy made his way to the entrance and up the steps, surrounded by the bright lights – he found the smell of the opera house intoxicating. He was, however, feeling very unwell and weaker and weaker and realised that this trip had made him very sick. As he made it into the foyer of the Alhambra he collapsed and died but not before taking in the decoration and interior grandness and glamour of the building.

The theatre staff were so shocked and upset by this tragic little visitor that they arranged a funeral for him, never knowing who he was.

The ghost of Billy is often seen sitting on the front step of the theatre and in the surrounding streets, but he is not the spirit of when he died but that of Billy before he was crippled and disabled by disease. So look out for the cheeky little lad when you are around this area of Brighton and give him a smile if you do!

Haunting Hooves at the Arcadia also known as The People's Picture Palace, Lewes Road

In 1910 The People's Picture Palace on Lewes Road was one of Brighton's first cinemas offering over 450 seats. It was previously known as the Arcadia Theatre of Varieties where the famous Harry Houdini appeared. However in the early 1900s this building was actually stabling for Tilley's Horse Bus stables. The sound of hooves clopping up the street would be heard in the interval at the cinema and also when the building was in use as a theatre. Many say that it went back to the times when the building was used as stables for the horses which pulled the buses and somehow that the building was haunted by the sounds of the past.

Disfigured Spirits at the Canterbury Music Hall, Church Street

Attached to the Brewers Arms and formerly the Apollo, the music hall was enlarged and refurbished with galleries and boxes and was a luxurious place to perform. It dominated the Brighton Music Halls until 1864 until it closed in 1868. During its high years this was one of the places that performers flocked to find work. The manager, however, was very strict about the age of his performers and once they started to look older they were not required any more and found it difficult to find work. There was always a younger, prettier singer to take the place of a middle-aged lady; competition was very high and ladies would try to stay younger looking for longer. No one wanted to be told they looked too old! With this desire to stay looking young came the back-street houses and shops offering unique treatments that would keep the ladies in the work that they so wanted. Many of these 'clinics' were not regulated and horrendous disfigurements occurred. Some people preyed on these victims of society and one such clinic offered an acid bath to take off layers of skin – so naive were the woman that they paid large sums for this procedure which literally took the skin off their bones; many died from the shock it gave to their systems.

Some of these poor victims are said to haunt the music hall where they had been most happy in a last-ditched attempt to work there and be around beautiful people again. Of the most notorious 'doctors' offering acid treatment was a failed gentleman actor who decided to make these women ugly in revenge for his lack of success.

Spirits of his victims still haunt the area around Church Street and are sometimes seen by members of the public. Many of them lurk down side alleyways and passageways knowing that they are too horrific to be seen. They live in the shadows, such a sad end for these actresses who were once beautiful. A harsh price to pay for wanting to stay young looking.

Poltergeist Activity at the Corn Exchange

Brighton's Corn Market was built in 1868 and was renamed the Corn Exchange. This building has led an interesting life and has had numerous stars grace its stage. Poltergeist activity has also been present here for many years but little notice is really taken of it anymore as it causes no harm or hurt in anyway.

It is particularly in the bar area that ghostly activity has been noted, where glasses fall, breaking and explode when no one was near them. The poltergeist also plays naughty tricks in the ladies toilets and it has been known to flush the toilets when people have been using them!

Spirit of the Wardrobe Mistress at the Empire Theatre of Varieties, No. 16 New Road

Costing £17,000 to build in 1892 and demolished in 1967, an office block now stands on its site, however the story of past hauntings at the old Empire Theatre is one which will last for centuries.

The story dates back to when there were many theatres in Brighton which brought jobs to an area where unemployment was high and interesting good work was hard to come by. Today, behind-the-scenes jobs are far more technical and complex than they used to be although the principle of them is very much the same.

One job which has mainly remained the same is the role of the wardrobe mistress and costume designers who source, find the materials and make the costumes for many stars each week. It entails checking costumes are from the correct period, the right size, colour, style and design, making sure they are cleaned and stored correctly and carrying out any repairs before they are used again. Many think that the job of the wardrobe mistress is glamorous with stars trying on and buying magnificent gowns all the time. Part of the job is glamorous but there are also the laborious tasks that come with any job. However year after year the vacancies in theatres across the country draw an increasing number of interested applicants. Some seeking a job within the theatre world may hope to meet the famous and others wish to let their creative side free.

Agatha Starr came from a small farming village in southern Ireland and travelled to Brighton in 1893 in search of work. She came from a family of seamstresses and had great style and flair in her blood for dress sense. She had heard of the opportunities for people with her skills in the new resorts on the coasts of England and left her home in the hope of finding a job. Agatha was snapped up by the Empire Theatre in Brighton which opened its doors in 1892. She was offered a position almost instantly and started work as wardrobe assistant; within a year was promoted to head wardrobe mistress. Agatha loved her work – it was just what she had dreamed of and she had never been so happy. Famous people asked her to make elegant gowns and others asked her advice about materials and colours of lace and rich velvets. She loved preparing for a large performance, lining up costumes, hats and accessories and helping out in any way that she could. However she missed her home and family terribly. She never took any holiday and so when she received notice from her mother than her younger brother was very ill, she was allowed three months leave and told that her job would still be there for her when she returned. Agatha caught the ferry back to Ireland and couldn't wait to see everyone and give them the gifts of old costumes and bits and pieces from the theatre world. However as soon as she arrived home she was very aware of how sick her brother was. His little face shone with happiness as soon as he saw his beloved sister. Agatha spent as much time as she could with him knowing that this would be the last time she would see him alive. She told him of her life at the theatre and about the resort of Brighton. She promised that one day she would take him and introduce him to her acting friends and he was in his element.

Agatha was very sad when the time came for her to return to her work in Brighton. She promised that she would be back to see them all very soon. She caught the ferry back as she did the very first time to England, however, as the ship was about halfway across the sea there was an intense storm and the boat collided with another vessel and started to sink. Within moments it had taken in vast amounts of water and was submerging rapidly into the cold icy water.

It wasn't long before all trace of the ship was gone. No one at the theatre could believe it when they received the news and neither could Agatha's family. Her brother took a turn for the worse on hearing of his sister's death and he died that very night in his sleep. Everyone who had known her was numb with the pain as she was an enchanting and creative person whom everyone adored.

Her ghost lingered on in the Empire and backstage workers would say they had seen a figure who looked the image of Agatha going about her business as she used to, but of course they could not have as she was dead. Actors and actresses getting ready for their performances were just not the same when Agatha wasn't there – she knew just exactly what they wanted and needed and everything was so organised. Without her, things were just not the same. However quite often someone would be looking for something and as if by magic it would appear or something that was broken would mysteriously repair itself. The happy spirit of Agatha Starr lived on at the Empire for many years.

Creepy Feeling at the Gaiety Theatre, Park Crescent Place
Opened in 1876 at a cost of £5,000, this theatre was built in the style of a circus. Renamed the Gaiety in 1890 it became notorious for lurid productions; increasing

competition led to its closure in 1900. The theatre became Fryco's mineral water factory in 1901 until it was demolished in 1930. Devonian Court now occupies the site and a fragment of the theatre wall is still visible.

A friendly spook was said to reside in the theatre shortly before its closure and would love to make its presence known to the people attending the building. It was often reported that they would sense someone behind them and feel their hats being removed and put on back to front.

Feline Phenomena Haunt the Globe Inn Music Hall, Edward Street

In 1851 Tom Swann and Leonard Burton took over the site adjacent to the Globe formerly occupied by Betty's Circus in 1841; it then became Burton's Music Hall. It sadly burnt down in 1853 and was rebuilt as the Sussex Music Hall, reopening in 1856. During its short life as the music hall it is said to have been frequently visited by a large black cat who became a lucky mascot for the cast. When the hall closed the cat lost his home and no one knows where he went; today a ghost cat is often seen rushing in front of people or just asleep on one of the hall's steps.

The Theatre Royal, North Road

The Theatre Royal dates back to the early 1800s when it was one of the finest theatres outside of London. It could seat over 1,100 people and became one of the most established theatres in the area. Today seating is limited to around 900 but it still remains a beautiful and magnificent building and is probably one of the best known of Brighton's theatres. Next door is the Colonade Bar, another magical place to catch a drink before or after a show, where the visitor can enjoy the beautiful décor and atmosphere with its black and white photos of the stars giving an insight into a more glamorous world. It was once said, although I am not sure how true this is, that near the present toilets there was once a secret adjoining passageway between the theatre and the bar used by performers who wanted a drink when feeling nervous before a show!

The theatre is said to be haunted, and the ghostly tales are known by many. One of them is the ghost of an old doorman who dedicated his whole working life to the Theatre Royal and was a well-known figure day and night, welcoming and greeting people. He always looked smart in his uniform and made visitors welcome to the establishment. It was said that he died of a broken heart when it was suggested that he should retire at quite an old age. His life was the theatre. However his happy spirit has chosen to linger on there with visitors today reporting being greeted by a smart, professional gentleman in regal uniform; no one fitting his description was employed at the theatre at the time of the reported sightings. He continues to greet people and is still regularly seen at the theatre today.

The Spirit of the Landlord at the Tierney Royal Picture Theatre

This theatre dates back 200 years and was once the site of the Tierney Arms pub. In 1916 it became the Picturedrome, in 1919 the Majestic Cinema and in 1920 was renamed the Devonshire Cinema. It finally closed to film in 1922. In 1927

Theatre Royal, Brighton, where theatre-goers are often met by a ghostly doorman. (© Jonny White)

it became known as Brighton Boys' Club and the Brighton Youth Centre in the 1950s. It goes to show that you can never really tell what history a building holds simply by looking at it. However one thing which does seem to be consistent through the history of this building is the ghostly phenomena. People who worked at the Majestic and the Devonshire told me of strange goings-on especially late at night when they were cleaning, locking up or doing security checks. Often they would find their cleaning equipment in a different place to where they had left it or lights they know they had turned off being switched back on, but no one felt spooked in any way and looked on it as mischievous poltergeist activity.

The story behind this behaviour goes back to when the building was the Tierney Arms and the landlord was a well-known character in the local vicinity. His wife was jealous of his popularity with local people and would often try and put him down by moving the tools of his trade or trying to disrupt his work in any way possible. But these strange acts did not change the landlord and he just carried on as normal, knowing deep down that it was the jealous work of his wife.

She continued her strange goings-on in the hope that her husband would quit his job and give her all his attention, but the more he worked the more it drove her crazy until it was said that it drove her completely mad and she had to be sent to a hospital for those with illnesses of the mind.

Today the unexplained goings-on are put down the landlady's strange behaviour.

The Curse of the Grand Theatre of Varieties, North Road

Circus proprietor Frederick Ginnett opened the theatre in 1891 at a cost of £13,000 and it became a prime venue for Brighton. It was constantly packed with crowds wishing to be part of this new lifestyle which was sweeping along the resort towns. It was converted to the Grand Cinema in 1931 and closed down in 1955. In 1957 it was converted to Funnell's furniture factory which burnt down in 1961.

Gresham House now occupies the site. It is said that some sort of curse was put on the site by the family of a trapeze artist who fell to his death whilst working at the Grand. Until Gresham House was built on the site no business survived very long and unfortunately burned to the ground. However someone must approve of what is going on now as it seems that the curse has been lifted.

Creepy Candles at the Hippodrome Theatre of Varieties, Middle Street

In 1897 there was a large ice-skating rink on this site which was popular and unique to the town. In 1902 successful Tom Barrasford converted the rink into a musical hall and since then it has become one of Brighton's main variety venues with the Beatles and the Rolling Stones amongst those who have performed there. Today it is a Mecca bingo establishment.

Many patrons of the venue believe the building to be haunted, in particular the ladies toilets.

During its time as a theatre it was said to have been haunted by phantom candle light! Candles have long been a traditional method and source of light dating back to the Roman period when they were developed to light buildings. Tallow was the main ingredient and was acquired from beef suet.

It wasn't until the Middle Ages that beeswax was used. Beeswax candles were very upmarket compared to ones made of tallow and could only be afforded by the wealthy. Paraffin was introduced in the 1850s making candle production even cheaper. The light bulb was produced in 1879 and candle making declined. In the early 1900s the candle became popular once again and production grew in vast quantities. Today candles are mass produced and made mainly from paraffin, although beeswax candles are still made.

Candles have long been associated with spooky settings and large gothic houses and there is nothing more creepy than sitting round an open fire in candlelight and telling ghost stories!

It is considered bad luck to use candles in the theatre and anyone carrying a candle backstage is in grave danger of being thrown out probably because of the number of theatres that have been burnt to the ground by unexplainable fires possibly caused by carelessness with candles.

The Hippodrome has a strange phenomenon; after dark there has sometimes been seen a strange flickering of light – a small flame is seen suspended in the air just as though someone is carrying a candle in a candleholder – but no figure is ever seen! It has long been reported but no one seems to know who it is. Perhaps

Hippodrome Theatre, Brighton has seen poltergeist activity for many years.

Flickering candlelight has haunted the Hippodrome for years. (© Jonny White)

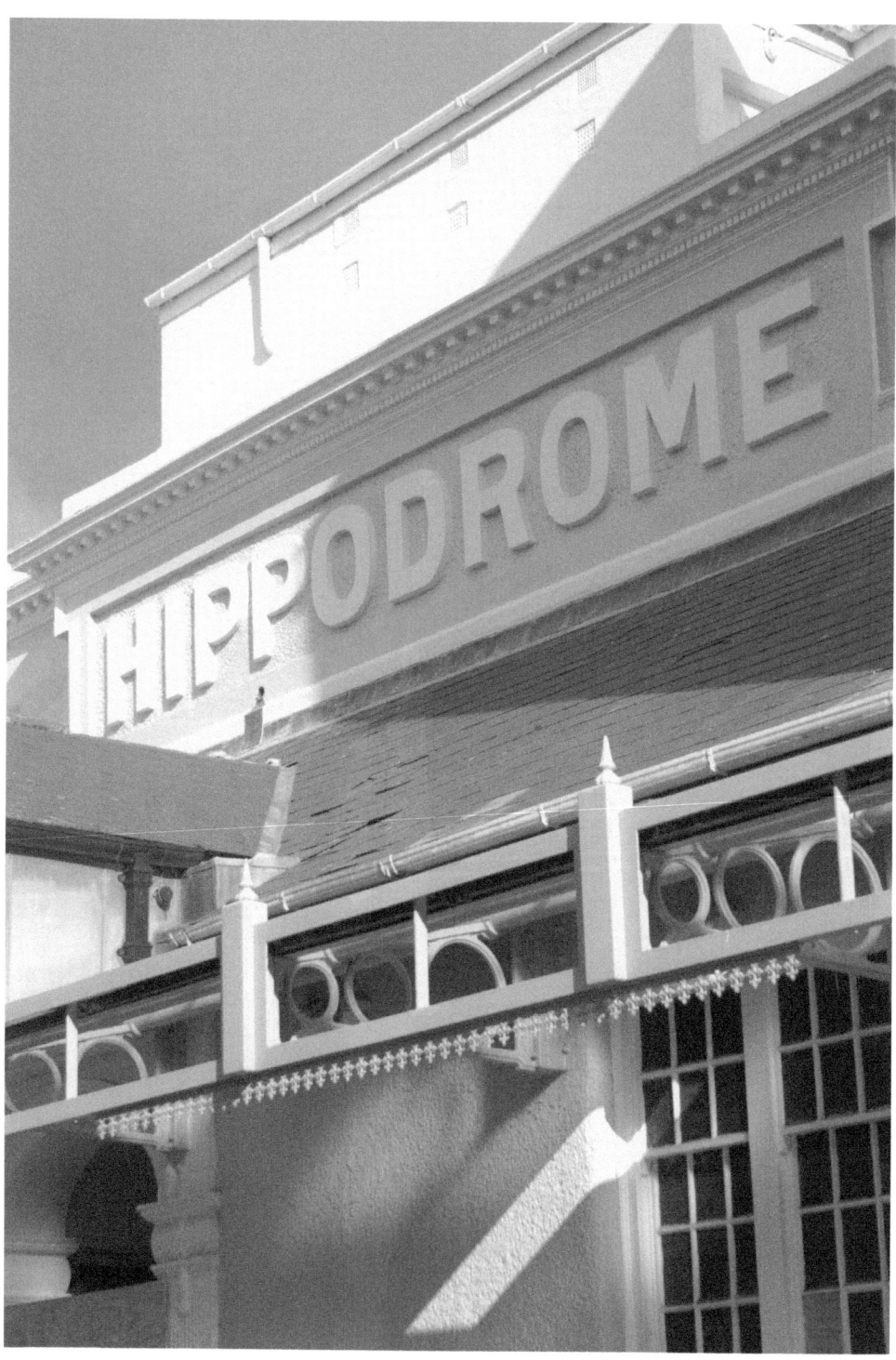

Hippodrome Theatre, Brighton has seen poltergeist activity for many years. A dear little spirit is seen here – a young girl in Victorian dress is often seen sitting on the stairs.

it is the spirit of someone who was banned from the theatre for carrying a naked flame. Perhaps he has come back to seek revenge for being thrown out all those many moons ago?

Lamb and Flag Inn, Cranbourne Street

This was one of many small concert rooms that encouraged local talent in Brighton and dates from 1858/59. Many locals flocked to the inn if they thought that they may have a chance of becoming a star. It was a popular venue for talent spotters of the day and people knew that if they were good they may well be seen and transformed into a rich and famous person!

Today it is known as the Easy Bar where a ghostly phenomenon has made its home. The figure of a smartly dressed man in a tall black hat is sometimes seen sitting in a corner as though observing the people and place around him. He is said to be the spirit of a gentleman talent spotter from the times when it was the Lamb and Flag Inn. The talent spotters would sit in the corner of the inn and watch as new acts and local people performed, sometimes finding a potential star. This ghost often lingers here, causes no harm and doesn't stay for long. Perhaps he is still on the look out for a new star.

Nightingale Theatre

To me the Nightingale Theatre is one of the most beautiful and attractive buildings in Brighton. It was originally built in the 1880s as the Railway Hotel. Ideally situated opposite Brighton Railway Station, its striking façade would greet many a visitor from other towns and cities looking for somewhere to stay. It was one of many hotels which sprung up at this time to cope with the influx of visitors to the town.

Many think the building overbearing and crudely designed but I think it adds to the appeal and atmosphere of its historical background. Today the Nightingale offers an ideal arts venue in a perfect location and is enjoyed by many.

It is said to be haunted by the ghost of a young girl who came to the Railway Hotel not long after it opened. Emily Coalthorpe was the fourteen-year-old daughter of a tailor and his wife from south east London and had been sick all her life with breathing problems and chest pains. Her parents heard that sea air had life-giving properties to those who were fragile and they wanted to do the best they could for their daughter so they joined the many others who swarmed to the resort. The family had never experienced anything like this – clean air, clean streets, flowers, trees and the sea. People were enjoying themselves, unlike the people the Coalthorpes met during their day-to-day lives in London, many of whom were miserable, dirty and often drunk. Brighton was like heaven and the Coalthorpes believed a month by the sea would cure their daughter. To begin with all was well and it was as though Emily had been given a new lease of life – she could walk along the prom without her pains in her chest, she could go to concerts, walk along the pier like other people and even bathe in the sea.

Above and opposite: The beautiful Nightingale Theatre, Brighton.

However things took a turn for the worse after one trip to the beach when the weather suddenly became quite cold and it was feared that she had caught a chill. She took to her bed and her family trusted that after a few days' rest she would be back to normal, but three days later, exhausted and fragile, she died. Doctors said that Emily's condition had not really changed much since arriving by the sea but all the enjoyable experiences had made her feel better and that in itself was a tonic. She had worn herself out but at least she had been happy. As she was dying her parents told her that she would always be their beautiful little nightingale – perhaps this is how the theatre acquired its name.

To this day the ghost of little Emily lingers on and has been observed sitting at the top of the stairs. Those lucky enough to have seen her have described a girl in Victorian dress and buttoned boots with her hair in plaits. She has even been known to acknowledge patrons at the theatre who feel no fear when they see this dear little spirit.

Ghostly West Pier Theatre

This poor structure has been left to fall in the sea and is desperately in need of some tender loving care. It is sad to see what was once such a beautiful and stunning building being neglected in such a way. It opened in 1866 purely as a walking platform for the Victorian middle classes to be seen as they strolled along whilst gazing out to sea. The bandstand was constructed in the 1870s and during the early 1880s a pavilion was added which was turned into a theatre in 1903. The West

Pier's popularity grew and offered plays, concerts, ballets and panto to thousands every year.

Sadly its decline began with the advent of the package holiday, drawing people abroad and offering new and exciting experiences which British seaside resorts could not compete with.

More recently severe storms, vandalism and arson have taken their toll on the pier – once these piers have gone, they can never be replaced.

The Pier Theatre used to have its own ghost. Actors and actresses had reported seeing a well-dressed gentleman sitting in the audience during rehearsals, usually in the same place, but never speaking or acknowledging anyone. It is said that he was one of the theatre's designers who found immense joy seeing the pleasure which his creation brought to so many people. He would truly be deeply saddened if he could see the building as it is today.

North Street Theatre
This was the first purpose-built theatre in Brighton constructed in 1773 by a local builder at a significant cost. He wanted to create an attraction as great as the acts that would be held there. From the beginning it seemed doomed; some parts had to be rebuilt and architects' drawings were incorrect. Once it opened it was not the huge success the builder had hoped and no one seemed to want to appear there. Many of the established theatres in Brighton were able to offer more attractive pay and runs.

Brighton Pier.

West Pier, Brighton where the past lingers on in its skeletal remains.

Brighton Palace Pier – are you brave enough to ride its haunted ghost train?

Many say that the theatre owner was too desperate for his theatre to be a success and so gave away many tickets hoping that people would want to revisit, however even this didn't seem to work. It is said that he made a fatal mistake in giving out complementary tickets. There is a long tradition or superstition in the theatre which says free tickets should never be given away before one has been sold. It appears that North Street Theatre was doomed before it had really begun and after only sixteen years of business it was in financial ruin and had to close. Some say it never made any money at all; financial ruin broke the owner and it is said that he went crazy – he was seen running naked into the sea one winter's night at midnight and was never seen again.

Ghostly phenomena of the feline variety have been seen stalking and lurking round corners and some people have reported feeling something brush against them as they have walked around the building, on the stairs or rushing in the opposite direction. It is thought to be the friendly spirit of a black cat who belonged to the theatre's caretaker. It followed its master everywhere, even to work, and would often sleep at the theatre overnight if his master was working there. Known as 'Blackie' people visited the theatre to see the black cat who was considered a lucky mascot. Its happy spirit lived on for many years after its master passed away; it is said that they both died on the same day at the same time. The shadow of a small figure is still seen in the theatre today believed to be the cat, keeping guard and making sure that no funny business happens today just as his master would have done all those years ago.

Haunted Ghost Train, Palace Pier Theatre

The Palace Pier in Brighton was one of the last to be built in England and was purely designed for the pleasure of holidaymakers to make their stay by the sea more perfect. It took ten years to complete and boasted second to none facilities catering for all – amusements, refreshments, smaller pavilions for reading and smoking, swimming, boat trips and an Oriental Theatre. During severe weather the theatre was badly damaged but in 1984 it was decided to restore it. The remainder of the theatre was dismantled and stored away until rebuilding started. However, the ornate original pieces disappeared and have never been found.

An amusement arcade is now on the site and it is unknown whether the Oriental Theatre will ever be rebuilt.

Sometimes on a stormy night when the sky is illuminated by lightning and the moon shines down on the pier, you may be lucky enough to catch a glimpse of the pier with the Oriental Theatre intact in its former glory. Does this prove that buildings have souls and spirits?

Today Brighton Pier is still popular and is visited by thousands of visitors each year. One of its much-loved attractions is its magical ghost train, created in 1862. It was displayed at fairgrounds on piers throughout Britain as a small theatre with puppets, unlike today's ghost trains. Crowds at this time were obsessed with ghost stories and anything sinister – the middle classes often had nothing to do

Duke of Yorks Cinema. Aromas of the building's history as a brewery linger on.

in the evenings and so story telling was a popular pastime. A labyrinth of hair-raising spectacles was on show to delight those brave enough to step on board its carriages.

During the 1950s there was an increased popularity in ghost trains with skeletons used to add creepiness to the show. The magic was the illusion of creating a spooky atmosphere – participants were able to feel and see scary objects and some said that the shows were so realistic they felt as though they had died and were surrounded by real ghosts!

Brighton Pier's ghost train is said to be haunted – strange but true! Over the years unexplainable goings-on have regularly occurred mostly when the show/ride was turned off. The mechanism of the ride is regularly checked by workmen and a number of them have been so afraid they have refused to work alone. They each tell of an experience which they will never forget. Due to the technical features of the ride they have to work without electric lighting and can only take torchlight to certain parts. They have reported brand new torches, in full working order, dimming and the light fading suddenly when they arrive at a certain area of the ride. Although they are working alone, they feel as if there is someone or something else there, watching them. Footsteps are heard – but no one is seen. Some workmen have only lasted one day and even contractors have refused to go back. It is said that this is the ghost of someone of a nervous disposition who went

Duke of Yorks Cinema, Brighton – the cinema with the famous black and white legs.

on the very first ride back in Victorian times and died of the shock of seeing the ghosts! Their ghost has come back to seek revenge!

Brewery Ghost at the Duke of Yorks Cinema

Today this is one of the best-known cinemas in Brighton; maybe not because of the exceptional films being showcased here but more to do with the strange addition to the outside of the building on the edge of the roof area. For on the top of the front wall is a pair of black and white stripy legs poking up into the air! This unusual sight is well known and makes me smile whenever I see it.

The Duke of Yorks Cinema was the first purpose-built cinema of its kind. It was built in 1910 in Edwardian baroque style on the site of the Amber Ale Brewery and has been well preserved over the years. One of the original walls from the old malt house forms part of the auditorium of the present cinema.

Over the years the cleaning and security staff, working alone, have reported an overwhelming aroma of beer being brewed, only noticed when they working alone. The smell seems to ooze from the building itself – maybe the wall in the auditorium has something to do with it. Just before the Amber Ale Brewery was closed one of its young workers was tragically crushed to death by beer barrels one night when he was working alone. It was during an evening of extra work when he was crushed to death by falling barrels and he had no colleague to help him. The Ghost of Tim (as he has become known) has never been seen, but people know he is around when the smell occurs. Perhaps he is trying to prevent another accident. In his own way Tim is watching over the workers today and making sure that they are ok.

12

BATTLE

The Creepy Monk of Battle
Battle is a small, unique market town approximately five miles north of Hastings. It has a quaint, rural feel to it with traditional and independent shops and a weekly market.

The town is world famous for the Battle of Hastings of 1066. Battle Abbey dominates the town, standing at the end of the High Street. Built on the site of the battle by William the Conqueror, it was completed around 1094. Much of the abbey is still intact although the older parts have fallen into ruins. Some surviving buildings from the thirteenth and sixteenth centuries now form part of the Battle Abbey School. The site of its high altar is exactly where King Harold fell in action on Saturday 14 October 1066. Following the Dissolution of the Monasteries by Henry VIII between 1536 and 1541, it was almost completely destroyed.

Thousands of people visit the abbey and its grounds each year. In October re-enactments take place on the fields close to the abbey, and festivals are held to mark its history.

The town of Battle grew up around the abbey and the area became well known for its high-quality gunpowder produced at a mill along Powdermill Lane (now the rather grand Powdermill Hotel). It was famous for its watch and clock makers who were said to be 'second to none' compared to their colleagues in the city of London. During the First World War Battle acted as a refuge and use was made of the tunnels which joined the fields and cellars of the abbey.

One of the main centres in the High Street is the Battle Memorial Hall at No. 81 where regular meetings, clubs, private functions and productions are held. It is said to have its own ghostly monk.

Several years ago, a friend of mine was involved in an Elizabethan production at Battle Memorial Hall. During the dress rehearsal a cloaked figure was seen wearing what was described as an old-fashioned, brown-hooded monk's habit and simple sandals. The show's producer assumed he was part of the production but when he called the monk to join the rest of the cast, the figure stopped, stared and ran through the wall! Another time the monk was seen walking straight through the cast members and disappeared as if walking down some steps.

My friend decided to research who the monk may have been and the history of the area. She discovered that there were hidden tunnels deep beneath the Memorial Hall which joined the abbey. They were used by monks looking to escape the abbey's restrictive lifestyle where they could dabble in forbidden alcohol and other delights. She also discovered that one young monk was executed for committing one of the deadly sins and breaking his vows. It is this monk that is said to haunt the Memorial Hall today – perhaps he is still on the look out for further temptation! Battle Abbey plays host to open-air concerts throughout the summer during which a cloaked monk-like figure has again been seen running into one of the buildings through the walls!

Other local titles published by The History Press

Haunted West End Theatres
IAN SHILLITO AND BECKY WALSH

Take a trip behind the scenes of London's West End theatres to discover a spooky range of spectres following centuries of performances. With eye-witness accounts from actors, backstage and front of house staff, this book reveals the most haunted theatres in London. From the Lyceum to the Lyric, the astounding results demonstrate the historical links between spirits and the stage. It will captivate those interested in the shadowy past of London's haunted West End theatres.

978 0 7524 4521 2

Haunted Hastings
TINA LAKIN

Drawing on historical and contemporary sources *Haunted Hastings* contains a chilling range of ghostly phenomena. From the haunted staircase at the library in Claremont and the singing spectre of Hastings College, to the mysterious witch's footsteps in the Stag Inn and the phantom coach and horses that gallop up the High Street on a dark winter's night, this phenomenal gathering of ghostly goings-on is bound to mystify anyone interested in the supernatural history of the area.

978 0 7524 3827 6

Haunted Brighton
ALAN MURDIE

From heart-stopping accounts of apparitions, manifestations and related supernatural phenomena to first-hand encounters with polite ghosts, malign presences and poltergeists, this collection of stories contains both well-known and hitherto unpublished cases of hauntings from in and around Brighton. Drawing on historical, scientific and contemporary sources, *Haunted Brighton* contains a chilling range of ghostly phenomena including the ghost of Cary Grant at the Rottingdean Club to the Screaming Skull in the Lanes and the ghost who spelt out 'prove me innocent!' at Preston Manor.

978 0 7524 3829 0

Haunted Kent
JANET CAMERON

Haunted Kent contains spooky stories from around the county, including the hunchbacked monk at Boughton Malherbe, the black dog of Leeds and the well-known tale of Lady Blanche of Rochester Castle. This fascinating collection of strange sightings and happenings in the county's streets, churches, public houses and country lanes is sure to appeal to anyone wanting to know why Kent is known as the most haunted county in England.

978 0 7524 3605 0

If you are interested in purchasing other books published by The History Press, or in case you have difficulty finding any History Press books in your local bookshop, you can also place orders directly through our website

www.thehistorypress.co.uk